The Antelope

Or, Smoholler the Medicine Man

A Tale of Indian Adventure and Mystery

George L. Aiken

Alpha Editions

"This edition published in 2024

ISBN : 9789367244845

Design and Setting By
Alpha Editions
www.alphaedis.com
Email - info@alphaedis.com

As per information held with us this book is in Public Domain. This book is a reproduction of an important historical work. Alpha Editions uses the best technology to reproduce historical work in the same manner it was first published to preserve its original nature. Any marks or number seen are left intentionally to preserve its true form.

Contents

CHAPTER I. THE SURVEYORS' CAMP. ....- 1 -
CHAPTER II. THE ARROW MESSAGE. ....- 6 -
CHAPTER III. SMOHOLLER'S FIEND. ....- 12 -
CHAPTER IV. SMOHOLLER'S ANGEL. ....- 17 -
CHAPTER V. THE SCOUTING PARTY. ....- 22 -
CHAPTER VI. FINDING THE TRAIL. ....- 26 -
CHAPTER VII. A DESPERATE ENCOUNTER. ....- 30 -
CHAPTER VIII. THE PROPHET-CHIEF. ....- 34 -
CHAPTER IX. CONJURATION. ....- 37 -
CHAPTER X. ONEOTAH. ....- 42 -
CHAPTER XI. A SILVAN REPAST. ....- 46 -
CHAPTER XII. THE TREE-LADDER. ....- 51 -
CHAPTER XIII. MULTUOMAH. ....- 56 -
CHAPTER XIV. THE CHIEF'S BRIDE. ....- 60 -
CHAPTER XV. THE OLD HUNTER'S IDEA. ....- 65 -
CHAPTER XVI. HOLDING A COUNCIL. ....- 69 -
CHAPTER XVII. THE BOY EMBASSADORS. ....- 74 -
CHAPTER XVIII. THE WHITE LILY. ....- 79 -
CHAPTER XIX. ON THE WAY. ....- 84 -
CHAPTER XX. ONEOTAH'S MEMORIES. ....- 89 -
CHAPTER XXI. THE MYSTIC CAVERN. ....- 93 -
CHAPTER XXII. THE SEARCH IS ENDED. ....- 97 -

CHAPTER I.
THE SURVEYORS' CAMP.

The surveying party were camped upon the banks of the Columbia River, a short distance from the mouth of its confluent, the Yakima.

This party consisted of the two surveyors—Owen Blaikie, a bluff, middle-aged Scotchman, long since "naturalized" to this country, and Cyrus Robbins, a shrewd young Yankee, twelve United States soldiers under command of Lieutenant Charles Gardiner, detailed expressly from the nearest fort to protect the surveying party from predatory bands of Indians, an old hunter, generally known under the name of "Gummery Glyndon,"—his prefix of Montgomery having suffered this abbreviation at the hands of his associates—whose duty it was to act as guide, and keep the surveyors supplied with fresh meat; and two boys, the chain-bearers of the expedition.

These boys merit more than a passing notice here, as they are destined to play conspicuous parts in the events which were to follow the advance of the surveying party into the country of the Yakimas.

There was this peculiarity about them, that they were first cousins, and were both called Percy—Percy Vere and Percy Cute.

But despite their relationship and the similarity of their surnames, there was very little resemblance between the two.

Percy Vere was a slender youth, graceful and active, with a frank, honest face, and regular features, his hair being a dark chestnut, thick and curly, and his eyes a clear hazel, giving evidence of courage and decision of character in their glances. He looked quite picturesque in his coarse suit, with the trowsers tucked into high-topped boots, and his crispy curls straggling from beneath his broad-leafed felt hat.

Percy Cute was full a head shorter, and his figure was decidedly dumpish. He had a fat, good-natured face, light flaxen hair, and a laughing blue eye. Indeed, a grin appeared to be the prevailing expression of his features. He was sluggish-looking, and appeared like one who would not put forth exertion unless compelled to do so. He was dressed after the fashion of his cousin and comrade, with heavy boots, coarse trowsers, a striped shirt, with a broad collar, and a kind of roundabout, which was short for a coat, and too long for a jacket; and like him, he wore a revolver in a belt buckled around his waist, the pistol resting convenient to hand, upon his right hip, while on the left side the handle of a bowie knife made itself conspicuous.

All in this party carried arms, for the service was one of danger, and at any moment the emergency for their use might arise.

The boys were quite favorites in the party, the first by his frank, manly bearing, and accommodating spirit, and the other by his unvarying good nature, and the drollery in which he was so fond of indulging. His humor appeared to be inexhaustible, and his quaint manner of giving vent to it was irresistible.

In fact, Percy Cute had, at a very early age, been forcibly impressed by the antics of a clown in a circus, and his great delight had been to play clown from that eventful moment.

The culinary department of the expedition was attended to by a colored individual who combined the two functions of cook and barber for the party. He was a jolly little darky, but terribly afraid of the Indians. The fear of his life was that he might have his "wool lifted"—as the old hunter phrased it—before he got out of the wilderness. But he had one consolation even in this apprehension: he had, like a great many other barbers, invented a HAIR RESTORATIVE, which he considered infallible.

"Never you mind, boys," he would tell the soldiers, "if de Injines does gobble us, an' lift our ha'r, as Gummery says, I can make it grow ag'in—hi yah-yah! I jist kin!"

Whereupon he would exhibit a small bottle in a mysterious manner, adding, "Dar's de stuff dat can do it—you bet!" And then he would consign it to his pocket again.

This assurance afforded much amusement to the "high privates" of the party, who made a standing joke of the Professor's Hair Restorative—for Isaac Yardell had prefixed the word "Professor" to his name when he was a tonsorial artist in Chicago, before the spirit of adventure had seized upon him and led him after gold among the mountains of Montana.

Gummery Glyndon had brought in an antelope. Some of the soldiers had captured a few fish from the river, a fire had been built in the center of the camp, and preparations were going on briskly for the evening meal.

In this Isaac had four assistants, he having contrived to transfer the drudgery of his office, with true Ethiopian cunning, to others. A colored servitor will always shirk all the work he can. Thus two of the soldiers, a German named Jacob Spatz—Dutch Jake, was his camp name—and one Irishman, Cornelius Donohoe—Corney for short—were always available for services at meal-time, and the two boys—the Percys—collected the wood for the firing. By this arrangement Isaac had little to do but the cooking, which he performed to the entire satisfaction of the party.

Even the rough old hunter—Glyndon—a gaunt, grizzly man of fifty years of age, bestowed his meed of praise upon him.

"It don't matter what I bring in," he told Lieutenant Gardiner, "game, fish or fowl—antelope, mountain sheep, or b'ar meat, that Ike can just make it toothsome. These darkies take to cooking, 'pears to me, just as naturally as ducks do to water."

Ike had only one grievance in the camp, Percy Cute was continually playing jokes upon him. Such little pranks as putting powder in his pipe, nipping at the calves of his legs and imitating a dog's growl, and grasping his wool at night, and shouting a war-whoop in his ear, had a damaging effect upon Ike's temper, and he vowed deadly vengeance. But his vengeance never extended beyond a chase after Percy Cute with a ladle, with the laudable intention of administering a severe spanking; but in these onslaughts the redoubtable Isaac always came to grief; for, just as he would overtake the flying youth, Cute, with a nimbleness that his sluggish look and dumpy figure never led any one to expect, would suddenly fall upon his hands and knees, and pitch his pursuer over him. But as Isaac invariably alighted upon his head, he received no injury from these involuntary dives. A shout of laughter would herald his defeat, and he would pick himself up, and return to his camp-kettle, in a crest-fallen manner, swearing to himself until every thing got blue around him, and vowing that he would "fix him de next time, suah!"

These little episodes enlivened the camp, and nobody enjoyed them better than Gummery Glyndon. The old hunter had, generally, a morose look upon his seamed and weather-beaten countenance, and his hatred of every thing in shape of an Indian was well known.

Nor was the cause of that hatred a secret. He had been the victim of one of those forest tragedies so frequently enacted upon the frontier. It was the old story which has been told so often, and will be repeated until the extermination of the red-man—which has been going on slowly but surely for years—is completed.

While absent upon a hunting and trapping expedition, his cabin had been surprised, his wife and only child, a little girl some three years of age, cruelly murdered, and their mutilated remains consumed in the fire that destroyed his home.

A blackened ruin was all that was left of the spot that was so dear to him, and he found himself alone in the world, with only one thought in the future—vengeance upon the murderers.

In the drear solitude of that heart-sickening scene, and beside the ashes of all that he had treasured in the world, he breathed that vow of vengeance, which the lips of so many bereaved settlers in the Far West have sent up to heaven—death to the destroyers.

That was fifteen years before the time in which I introduce him here. In all those years he had pursued the Indians with a deadly malignity. He had taken part in every Indian war that had broken out, and the number of his victims had been many.

As the years passed away this feeling of vengeance grew fainter, and though he never spared an Indian who came against him with hostile intent, yet he did not go out of his way to seek for them, as he had done. The Yakimas were supposed to be the destroyers of his home and family, and against that nation he cherished an undying enmity. Yet circumstances had led him away from their country, to the hunting-grounds of the Apaches, with whom he had many encounters.

He had gladly accepted the service that would take him back to the land of the Yakimas. In all these years he had gained experience as a guide, in wood-craft, and as an Indian-fighter. No hunter of the plains bore a better reputation for skill, prudence, and knowledge of the Indians than Gummery Glyndon.

His face bore a somewhat morose expression, as I have said, but he was far from being a morose man. Indeed, there was quite a fund of dry humor in his disposition, which was an agreeable surprise to those who judged the man by his saturnine countenance.

Percy Cute was a particular favorite of his, and none in the party enjoyed the boy's drolleries more than he did. Indeed, both the boys were prime favorites with him, and often accompanied him upon his hunts. He looked upon them in the light of *proteges*, as he had got them their places in the expedition.

He had met them at Fort Benton, where they had come from Omaha up the Missouri river, on one of the steamboats that ply on that stream, and was rather surprised to hear what had brought them there.

Though partly led by a spirit of adventure, they had a mission, and one of some importance.

CHAPTER II.
THE ARROW MESSAGE.

Percy Vere explained this mission to the old hunter. His father had been missing for years. He was an eccentric character, and professed spiritualism, astrology, ventriloquism, and kindred sciences, dabbling a little in magic and chemistry. In fact, he was a universal genius—a jack-of-all-trades, and not doing well with any.

Percy's mother was a woman of ability and good sense, a first rate milliner, and her industry kept the wolf, which the father's eccentricities brought to the door, away. In other words, she was obliged to support herself and son, and often furnish money to the genius, who could not make it for himself with all his diverse talents.

He did not appear to be able to concentrate his forces so as to produce any good from them. He was full of wild theories and startling speculations, but he failed signally whenever he attempted to put them to an application.

His wife expressed her opinion of him freely one day, and told him she could no longer expend her savings in his wild schemes. He replied that it was the fate of genius to be misunderstood, that he was destined to be a great man, and she would live to see it; and having uttered this ambiguous prophecy, left her.

He did not return the next day, or the next—a year passed away without bringing Guy Vere home. His wife became alarmed at his prolonged absence. She reproached herself with being too harsh with him and having driven him away from her. He was a handsome man, and she had cherished a warm affection for him, which his eccentricities had not destroyed. She feared that she had driven him to commit suicide. But no tidings came of his death.

She was obliged to keep her little millinery shop going for the support of herself and son, and her sister's child, who being left an orphan, fell to her care. This was Percy Cute—who was just one year younger than his cousin, his mother having been so pleased with the name of her sister's child, that she had bestowed it upon her own.

The little shop prospered, and the boys grew in years. Mrs. Vere could not drive the image of her husband from her mind. If she could have satisfied herself that he was dead, she would have been more content, but she could not do that.

The impression among Guy's neighbors when he was at home, was that he was not in his right mind—"Luny," they called him.

But many years passed away before she got any tidings of the missing man, and then it came in a very vague shape.

Percy Vere got an Omaha *Herald* one day, which had been sent as an exchange to a St. Louis paper, and in it was the advertisement of an astrologer who called himself "Professor Guy."

He took it home to his mother, and said to her, "That's father!"

These words put her all in a flutter. She took the paper and scanned the advertisement eagerly.

"What makes you think so?" she asked.

"Father's name was Guy, and he was a 'professor' of astrology!"

She smiled. "He was a professor of almost everything."

"Suppose I go and see if it is my father," he suggested.

She pondered over this.

"Would you know him, do you think?"

"Oh, yes, if the picture you have in your locket is any thing like him."

"It was when it was taken."

She took out the locket, which she wore constantly around her neck, sprung it open, and regarded the two portraits it contained earnestly, for it held her miniature likeness as well as his.

"I have not changed much," she said, "and perhaps he has not, either. I should really like to know if he is alive. Suppose I was to write to this Professor Guy?"

Percy, who was a bright youth, shook his head dissentingly.

"If he is staying away of his own accord, it is no use to write to him to come back," he replied.

She breathed a sigh. "I suppose not," she said.

"But if I was to go after him and have a talk with him, I might prevail upon him to come back."

Mrs. Vere was impressed by these words, but she answered: "How could I trust you so far away from home?"

He smiled, and drew himself proudly up.

"Don't you think I am big enough to take care of myself?"

She surveyed his tall, graceful figure, with a mother's pride, saying:

"Perhaps; but you are so young."

"I'm seventeen, and I feel quite a man."

"But I don't like to trust you so far from home alone."

"Oh! I needn't go alone; Percy can go with me."

Mrs. Vere laughed.

"A great protection he would be—another boy like yourself!" she cried. "There, there—let us not talk any more about it."

But they did talk about it upon several occasions afterward, and Mrs. Vere's desire to hear from her missing husband overcame all other considerations, and she consented to Percy's request to go in search of him. She thought that the sight of his boy would induce him to return home.

Her business had proved prosperous, as I have said, and she was able to fit out the boys in good style. She hung the locket that contained her own and husband's likeness around her son's neck, and bade him a tearful "good speed."

The boys took passage upon a steamboat bound for Omaha, and steamed up the Big Muddy, as the Missouri is called by the dwellers on its banks, and reached that ambitious city in due season.

Upon making inquiries, Percy Vere learned that Professor Guy had found Omaha dull for the exercise of his profession, and had joined a party of adventurers—a mixture of hunters and gold-seekers—and gone with them to Fort Benton.

The very eccentricity of this proceeding was a convincing proof to Percy that this Professor Guy was indeed his father So he wrote to his mother, and then he and Percy Cute sailed up the river in one of the light-draught steamboats.

They reached Fort Benton without misadventure, but here, instead of being at the end of their journey, they found it was just the starting-point. The party to which the Professor had attached himself had taken the trail that led into the wilderness, and it was necessary to follow it, or abandon the search.

Percy Vere chose the former alternative, for he could never think of the latter, and Percy Cute was always of his way of thinking—in fact, thinking was irksome to his sluggish nature.

"I just tumble to any thing you say," he told his cousin. "Follow your leader—that's my maxim. You lead and I'll follow. Say! we might have some high old fun among the Injuns, and bears, and things. Let's invest in a revolver and bowie-knife, and travel on our muscle!"

So Percy Vere, filled with a true spirit of boyish adventure, wrote his intentions to his mother, and he and Cute made their preparations for a journey into the wilderness.

At this juncture of affairs they made the acquaintance of the old hunter, Gummery Glyndon. They told him their story, (or rather young Vere did, for he was the spokesman on all occasions) and he promised to aid them, and fulfilled his promise by attaching them to the surveying party, though in the capacity of chain bearers; but the boys did not mind that.

Such an opportunity to penetrate into the Indian country was not to be neglected, and the first Percy, who was treasurer, wished to husband their means, for there was no telling how long their search might last, or whither it would lead them.

They made rapid journeys at first, as a portion of the "Northern Pacific Railroad" had already been surveyed, and they were to take it up at, or near, that point, where it was to connect in a south-easterly direction with the "Union Pacific."

As they passed the different Government forts their escort was changed, until they were joined by Lieutenant Gardiner and his squad, from Fort Walla Walla. He was to remain with them until they were through the Yakima country.

Hitherto their journey had led through the land of the Nez Perces, who were a friendly tribe, and they had been undisturbed; but when they made this new camp Gummery Glyndon told them they might now expect trouble from the Indians.

"There's three tribes through here," he said, "and there ain't much choice between 'em. There's the *Cayuses*, the *Yakimas*, and the *Umatillas*—a pesky set of murdering thieves the lot of 'em. They all belong to the great Snake Nation, I believe—red sarpints, every mother's son of 'em."

When he returned from his hunt he told them that he had seen "Indian sign."

"There's Injuns watching us, and we shall hear from them," he said. "We'll have to keep a sharp watch to-night, or they'll stampede our animals."

The lieutenant and the surveyors did not neglect this warning. They had great confidence in the old hunter's judgment.

When the supper was disposed of the camp was placed in as good a condition of defense as the locality would permit. The ground had been well selected; it was a little grove on the river's bank, a kind of oasis among the cliffs, which rose beetling upon either side, precipitously, and, apparently, inaccessible. These cliffs were some distance—a long rifle-shot—from the little grove, and a kind of rocky valley lay between them, devoid of vegetation in many places, where the hard rocks cropped up. Through this valley must the foe come, or else risk their necks, or a plunge into the river, by attempting to skirt the cliffs.

The horses belonging to the party were secured in the grove. In the center of the grove, in a kind of natural fireplace formed by the rocks, the fire had been built, and its red embers were still glowing. Two sentinels were posted at either extremity of the camp. Around the fire the hunter, the surveyors, and the lieutenant were stretched in easy attitudes, enjoying their pipes of tobacco—the great luxury of the wilderness.

A short distance from them the two boys reclined upon a mossy bowlder, listening to their conversation.

The sun had sunk, and the glorious twilight of that western land was upon them. The scene was of calm tranquillity. But that tranquillity was broken in a singular manner.

There came a hurtling sound in the air, and an arrow descended, apparently from the heavens, and stuck quivering in the turf at Lieutenant Gardiner's head.

All started and grasped their weapons, instinctively, for the trusty rifles were close at hand.

"An attack?" cried Gardiner.

"No—a message. See, there's a scroll upon the arrow," answered Gummery. "Read it."

He threw some brush upon the coals which speedily burst into a flame. Lieutenant Gardiner undid the scroll of bark from the arrow, and spread it open. It contained characters which he had no difficulty in deciphering, for they were written in English.

> "White men, begone! If you advance further into the land of the Yakimas, certain destruction awaits you.
>
> "SMOHOLLER, THE PROPHET."

CHAPTER III.
SMOHOLLER'S FIEND.

"What does this mean?" added Lieutenant Gardiner, having read this singular scroll aloud.

"A game of bluff!" answered the irrepressible Percy Cute. "Let's see him, and go two better!"

"It'll be more than a bluff game," rejoined Gummery Glyndon, shaking his head gravely. "This means business. It's a notice to quit, and if we don't take it, these Injuns will do their best to put us out."

"Rub us out entirely, I guess you mean," cried Surveyor Robbins, laughingly. "But we won't take the back track on such a notice as that. Who is this Smoholler?"

"Yes, that's what I want to know," chimed in Blaikie and Lieutenant Gardiner.

"I have heard tell of him, though I never met him," replied Glyndon. "He's a great gun among the Injuns hereabouts. He's a kind of red Brigham Young—calls himself a Prophet, and has started a new religion among the red-skins."

"What is this religion like?"

"That's more than I can say; though, from what I've heard, there appears to be a deal of trickery about it. He's a great Medicine-man, and can raise the Old Boy, generally. He has his familiar fiends, and makes 'em appear to his followers whenever he likes. He works miracles, and all that sort of thing. And when he predicts the death of any one, they just go, sure pop, at the time mentioned."

"A singular man, this," remarked Lieutenant Gardiner, thoughtfully.

"He's more smart than sing'lar; he just keeps these benighted heathen right under his thumb. They don't dare to say their souls are their own when he's around."

"Where did he come from?"

"He is said to be a Snake Indian of the Walla Walla tribe. He started a village on the river, above here, at a place they call Priest's Rapids, and his followers increased like magic. He is said, by the Nez Perces, to have a couple of thousand of believers, renegades from all the other tribes in this region, and he can put three hundred fighting men in the field, and then the Cayuses, Yakimas and Umatillas all stand in dread of him, and wouldn't dare to do any thing else but join him in a war against the whites if he called on 'em. I believe he's got a reg'lar stronghold at Priest's Rapids."

"Is it named so on his account?" asked Robbins.

Glyndon shook his head dubiously.

"I s'pose so, but I couldn't say for sure. I don't know the place; was never up there."

"What kind of a place is it—did you ever hear?"

"Oh, yes. It is north of the Oregon line, and is a great place for salmon-fishing. The Injuns have a great time catching 'em in the season."

"This Smoholler, then, is a kind of independent chief among the other tribes?"

"Yes; and his tribe is a conglomeration of all the other tribes, and the pick of 'em, too. They are called Smohollers by the other Injuns, but there's Cayuses, Yakimas, Umatillas, Modocs, Snakes, and Piutes amongst them."

"A mongrel set!"

"But tough customers to deal with."

Lieutenant Gardiner turned to Percy Vere.

"You and your chum send the sentinels in to me, and take their places—young eyes are sharp."

The two boys, who had been listening attentively to this conversation, obeyed at once, and the two sentinels soon appeared before the lieutenant. But they had not seen any one approach the camp, and were surprised to hear that an arrow had been shot into it.

Gummery Glyndon surveyed the nearest cliff critically. Its base was about a stone's throw from where he sat. The rising moon threw a silvery radiance upon its peak, disclosing an irregularity near its top, that looked like a cavity in its face, though it might have been only a shadow.

"It's my opinion the arrow came from there," he exclaimed, giving utterance to this thought suddenly.

All eyes were turned in the direction indicated.

"But how could any one get up there? A cat couldn't climb that. It's as steep and as smooth as a wall."

"Just you wait," returned the old guide, coolly. "If this Smoholler is the kind of man he's said to be, we ain't done with him yet. Just keep your weather eye peeled in the direction of that cliff, and have your rifles handy. That arrow was only the commencement. I saw plenty of Injun sign to-day, and there may be a hundred of Smoholler's braves beyond there. I opine that he is not going to let us travel much further into this country, if he can help it."

"But, man, what harm does our surveying do him?" asked Blaikie.

"He don't want any railroad through this country—all Injuns are down on railroads—sp'ils their hunting-grounds, and settles up the country. And the white settlers settle the Injuns. We've had a genteel notice to leave, and if we don't take it, we'll have 'em swarming round us like enraged hornets."

"You would not advise a retrograde movement?" asked Lieutenant Gardiner.

"Who said any thing about taking the back-track?" somewhat tartly rejoined Glyndon. "Did I? I never saw Injuns enough to back me down yet."

The lieutenant laughed, as he added:

"The suggestion of a backward movement came from me," he said, "and by so doing I am not afraid to have my courage called into question. Discretion is said to be the better part of valor. We appear to have reached a critical position here. Our party is small—nineteen in all, counting the two boys. If the Indians oppose us in force—and from what Glyndon says it seems that this Indian Prophet Smoholler can put three hundred warriors in the field—shall we be justified in advancing against such odds?"

The surveyors looked at Glyndon, but he was silent, gazing reflectively at the cliff, upon whose summit the moonbeams now played in a fantastic manner.

"I confess I don't like the idea of retreating," said Blaikie. "I don't want to be turned back by such a scarecrow as that."

"No more do I," added Robbins.

"I don't say go back, and I don't say go on," replied Glyndon, in his deliberate manner; "but I say, just hold on for a while here, where we are, until we can see how the cat jumps."

"How long will it be before the feline animal indulges in her gymnastic exercise, do you think?" asked Robbins.

"Before you can smoke another pipe," answered Glyndon. "I have an idea that something is going to happen right away—kind o' feel it in my bones. Get the men ready, leftenant—there's no telling what is— Hello! it's coming! Fireworks—by king!"

The amazement of the old hunter was shared by the whole camp, and the two boys came running in from their posts.

"See—see—look there!"

A strange fire issued from the face of the cliff, disclosing a little shelf or platform, backed by a cavity. From this cavity the fire came forth with crimson luster, and rose colored smoke rolled upward toward the heaven, obscuring the moon-rays.

The entire force of the whites clustered in front of the grove, clutching their rifles, and gazing with wondering eyes upon this singular sight, and exclamations burst spontaneously from their lips.

"Ach Gott! what ish dat?" cried the Dutch private.

"It's a volcayano!" explained the Irishman.

"It's the debble's fireplace!" mumbled Isaac, and his teeth chattered together with superstitious awe.

"It's some of Smoholler's deviltry!" said Glyndon.

The fire grew in intensity, and then a dark body seemed to grow up in the midst of it. A black, unearthly figure of a man, with eyes of fire, a tongue of flame, and livid horns projecting from his head, of a deep-red color.

"The devil!" was the cry that burst from the lips of the astonished whites.

He held what appeared to be a thunderbolt in his hand, and suddenly launched it like a javelin at the astonished gazers. It whizzed past Isaac's head, singeing his wool in its passage, and exploding at his heels, and the tonsorial professor sprawled upon his back with one heart-rending yell that evinced his firm belief that he had received his quietus.

"Fiend or man, I'll have a try at him!" cried Glyndon, and he took a rapid sight along the barrel of his rifle, and fired at the apparition on the cliff.

Two other rifles echoed his, for Blaikie and Robbins had impulsively followed his example. The three rifles sent forth their contents, and the smoke clouded their vision for a moment. But following the reports came an unearthly, soul-curdling laugh, and then something pattered down among them like heavy drops of rain.

Robbins stooped and picked up a round object that struck at his feet.

"Good heavens! here's my bullet sent back to me!" he cried.

These words sent a thrill through every heart. Isaac, still lying curled up in a heap where he had fallen, uttered a plaintive howl.

Percy Cute went to him.

"Are you dead, Ike? If you are, say so, and tell us where you would like to be buried," he said.

Isaac sat up on end, resenting this question.

"Glory!" he cried. "S'pose de debble had shot you, how would you like it?"

"Well, if I warn't hurt any more than you are, I shouldn't mind it much. Singed your wool a little, but your Hair Restorer will fix that all right, you know."

A roar of laughter followed this remark, and in the midst of it Isaac scrambled sheepishly to his feet.

CHAPTER IV.
SMOHOLLER'S ANGEL.

When the smoke of the rifles cleared away the fiend had vanished from the cliff, and the crimson light had died away. The silvery beams of the moon played hide and seek among the projections and depressions of the cliff's peak.

The gazers rubbed their eyes. What they had seen appeared to them already like a fantastic dream. But a new vision awaited them, a new wonder was to be presented to their eyes.

Another light began to glow from the cliff, but this time it was of a bluish tint, and the smoke that arose from it was white and fleecy. And this light grew dense, as the other had done, and assumed a form and shape—a shape of ethereal loveliness.

As the other vision thrilled the beholders with a kind of supernatural awe, so did this one excite their wondering admiration. It bore the shape they supposed an angel would wear.

The face was that of a girl, angelic in its beauty. Her long black hair floated in wavy masses upon her neck and shoulders, and was confined upon the forehead by a golden coronet in the center of which gleamed a diamond star, which emitted scintillating rays of light. Her arms and legs were bare, revealing their faultless perfection, and the alabaster purity of her skin. Her only garment was a long white tunic, of some snowy, fleecy fabric, confined at the waist by a golden cestus, which was studded with large rubies glittering with blood-red rays.

This angelic vision held in her right hand a kind of glittering dart. For a minute she transfixed their wondering gaze, then hurled the dart into their midst.

The fire around her grew more vivid, the volume of white smoke increased in density, obscured her figure from view, and then began to roll away. When the light of the fire faded and the smoke lifted from the face of the rock, the platform was vacant, the lovely vision had disappeared.

The surveying party gaze inquiringly into each other's faces. Lieutenant Gardiner expressed the general opinion by asking the hunter, Glyndon:

"What do you think of that?"

Glyndon shook his head dubiously.

"Did you ever see a girl as pretty as that one was?" he asked.

"Well, no, I can't say that I ever did," the lieutenant admitted, with a smile; "and if she is a human I should like to become better acquainted with her."

"All women have something angelic about them," said Glyndon, reflectively, and his voice had a strange touch of pathos to it as he spoke—"particularly when they are good and true women. I knew one once—an angel couldn't have had a better disposition, and she—" His voice broke here. "Well, well, the murdering red-skins sent her to heaven before her time!" he resumed, huskily. "And our little one went with her. Perhaps it was best so—but I've often thought I could have stood it better if she had been spared. Do you know, leftenant—it was an odd idea, but when I looked at that bright spirit-angel or whatever it was—up on the cliff yonder—I thought to myself, my little girl, maybe, looks just like that up in heaven."

The hunter turned away his head and wiped his eyes with the back of his bony hand. His hearers respected his grief for they knew the story of Glyndon's bereavement.

Percy Cute picked up the javelin and the dart, if they could be called by these names, for they were of singular construction, as we shall see anon.

"Here's the telegrams," he said; "they may tell us what the meaning of the diorama was. A piece of birch bark is wrapped around each."

"I must examine them," exclaimed Gardiner, taking possession of them. "Freshen up the fire, my boy, so we can have a little more light upon the subject."

"Better post the sentinels again," suggested Glyndon. "This deviltry may be only the forerunner of mischief."

"You are right. It behoves us to use every precaution."

Two other sentinels were posted, and then the balance of the party returned to the camp-fire in the grove, which the two boys had started into a blaze again.

One of the missiles hurled from the cliff was about four feet in length, the other two. The javelin was a stout stick of wood, apparently the shoot of a tree, about an inch in diameter, and was painted a blood-red color. It was blackened at one end, as if it had been loaded with some kind of firework, on the rocket principle. Around the middle of it a strip of flexible bark was secured by a leathern string.

The dart was formed of the bone of the fore leg of an antelope, and was gilded, as if by the application of that kind of gold-leaf known to printers as "Dutch Metal." This also had a strip of bark around it, but it was secured by a long black hair, soft and glossy, as if plucked from a woman's head.

"Funny gim-cracks, those," said Glyndon, as Lieutenant Gardiner unfastened the strips of bark.

"Yes; nothing very supernatural about these," he replied. "But let us see what Smoholler has to say this time."

He read the words upon the strip of bark taken from the javelin first:

"*Begone, or fear my vengeance!*"

"Good! So speaks the Fiend. Let's hear what the Angel has to say."

He read the second strip:

"*Depart in peace, and escape the destruction that threatens you.*"

Lieutenant Gardiner passed the pieces of bark to the surveyors for their inspection.

"Well, gentlemen, what do you think of this?" he asked.

Blaikie and Robbins examined the billets of bark curiously.

"There is one thing singular about this affair," said Blaikie.

"What is that?"

"These communications, like the one sent on the arrow, are written in English, either with a red pencil or a piece of red chalk, and apparently by the same hand, for the characters appear to be alike in each."

"There's nothing strange in that," said Glyndon. "Many Injuns have learned English from the numerous trappers and traders who have visited them at different times. A man as smart as this Injun Prophet must have had frequent dealings with the traders, and would be sure to get a smattering of the language."

"The man who wrote these communications had more than a smattering," returned Robbins. "This Smoholler is determined that we shan't run our railroad through his country, that's evident."

"Yes; and he has begun by trying to frighten us away."

"And if that don't do it, he'll try fighting us away next," responded Glyndon.

"Likely; but I don't scare worth a cent," rejoined Robbins. "This supernatural trickery may do among the Indians, but it won't answer with us. I'm going to survey this country in spite of Smoholler's angels or devils—though I wouldn't mind a closer inspection of the angel."

"Nor I," laughed Gardiner. "Girl or angel, she was certainly a vision of beauty. By Jove! suppose we search the cliff—we might find her there."

He started impulsively to his feet, under the excitement of this idea.

"I will go with you!" cried Percy Vere, always ready for an adventure.

"Count me in!" added Percy Cute; the idea was firmly impressed upon his mind that wherever Percy Vere went, he must go also.

"Sit down," said Glyndon, in his calm, deliberate manner. "You might as well attempt to find a needle in a haystack as search that cliff to-night. You'd only break your necks attempting it, and not find anybody, either. If there's a way up that cliff, they know how to get up and down it, and they won't stop there until we come to look for 'em. Wait until morning."

"They'll be gone then."

"They're gone *now*. If we could surround the cliff, it might have been of some use; but it joins the range beyond, as you can see, and they probably came from the back of it, through some crevice, which we can't see from here. I'll take a scout up that way in the morning, and see."

"My idea is to fortify our position here to the best of our ability, and await an attack, which is sure to come. We might repulse it here."

"You are right every way, leftenant," replied Glyndon. "This is a good p'int. While I take a scout to-morrow, just cut down a few of these trees, and make a breastwork. We can send to Fort Walla Walla for help if we are hard pushed; but I have an idea that if we pepper a few of Smoholler's followers, he'll get sick of it and let us alone. The railroad's bound to go through, and he can't help it. Perhaps I can get a talk with him, and convince him that we are not going within a hundred miles of his village. We'll see to-morrow. Now just sleep, all who want to. I'm going to keep an eye on that cliff for the balance of the night."

He took his rifle and walked to the edge of the timber; but his vigilance appeared to have been uncalled-for, as the quiet of the camp remained undisturbed through the night.

CHAPTER V.
THE SCOUTING PARTY.

In the morning, after partaking of breakfast, Gummery Glyndon prepared for his scout. During this, he was urged by Percy Vere to allow him and his cousin to accompany him.

The hunter was inclined, at first, to refuse this request, but on reflection, he consented.

"They are smart boys, both of 'em," he told himself, "and the surveyors always lend them their rifles when they go with me. I'd rather have them any time than the soldiers—these reg'lars ain't worth shucks in an Injun skirmish—it would be as good as three of us, and if the Injuns are thick among the hills, and I opine so, I shall want some help along. Yes, Percy, you can go."

These last words were uttered aloud.

The two boys were quite pleased at being permitted to join in the scout, and Blaikie and Robbins readily loaned them their rifles. The surveyors were well provided in this respect as each had a breech-loading, repeating rifle, besides the old-fashioned single-barreled, smooth bore one. The boys got the single-barreled ones, of course. But they were perfectly satisfied with them, and, by much practice, had gained considerable skill in their use.

"Do you know, Percy, I have an idea," said the elder boy, as they equipped themselves for the adventure.

"Have you? How does it feel? Tell me, so I'll know when I have one."

"Oh, pshaw! you are always at your joke. My idea is that Smoholler might give me some intelligence concerning my father."

"Very likely; but do you think it safe to trust yourself in Smoholler's power?" suggested Cute.

"Oh, no; but we might be able to hold a parley with him. I think he would prefer to arrange matters peaceably with us if he could. He must know that he can not drive back our party without considerable loss to himself."

"Yes, and from what I have heard old Gummery Glyndon say, I should fancy that these Indians don't like to take any risks. Do you know, Percy, I'd like to have a scrimmage with the red-skins. I think it would beat bear-hunting all hollow—Smoholler!"

Percy Vere laughed at this pun upon the Prophet's name.

"It might not be so funny as you imagine," he answered; "particularly if we should happen to get the worst of it, and you should have your hair lifted."

Percy Cute passed his fingers through his shock of flaxen hair, reflectively.

"I would not like to be obliged to experiment on Professor Ike's Restorative in that fashion," he said. "I'm afraid the soil is too poor for another crop, even with that help. But I'm not going to let any Indian take my top-knot if I can help it. I'll trust to my arms, while my powder and bullets last."

"And failing these?"

"My dependence will be in my legs."

"You are too fat to run fast."

"Not if a crowd of red-skins was after me. The way I could get over the ground then would be a caution to bedbugs."

Percy Vere laughed again.

"You'll do," he cried.

"You bet I will! Anybody's got to get up early to get ahead of my time."

"Are you ready, boys?" asked Gummery Glyndon, as he approached them.

"Ready and willing," responded Cute.

Glyndon took a critical survey of the boys, as they shouldered their rifles and joined him. Besides the rifle each was armed with a revolver—the large size called "navy"—and a bowie-knife, with a keen blade, six inches in length, and a stout horn handle. A serviceable weapon for a close encounter, and also serving the purpose of a hunting and table knife. Few travelers upon the plains and amongst the mountains of the Far West are without this useful article.

"You'll do," said Glyndon, shaking his head, approvingly. "Come on."

Lieutenant Gardiner followed them to the edge of the timber.

"How long do you intend to be absent?" he asked.

"I shall try to bring you in something for dinner," replied Glyndon. "I've got the boys, and so I can bring in considerable game, if we are lucky enough to find it. My idea is to go through the ravine, and skirt the cliff to the left there—where the deviltry was last night—looking for Indian sign by the way, and come back by the river's bank, if there's footing—if not, we'll get on some logs and let the tide float us down."

"A good idea," cried Gardiner, surprised by the mention of this expedient. "I should never have thought of that. You are cunning in devices."

"So are the Injuns," returned Glyndon, impressively. "Take care some of 'em don't come down on you that way while I'm gone."

"I'll look out for them; you'll find quite a fort here when you come back. I hardly think Smoholler will dare attack us here."

Glyndon took a critical survey of the situation, and shook his head in the manner he had when any thing met his approval.

"It's a good camping-ground," he said, "and you can hold it ag'in' a hundred Injuns, in *daylight*." He laid particular stress upon this word. "An open attack is what you can beat off without any trouble, but it's stratagem and trickery will bother you. But we can tell more about Smoholler when I come back. If he's got a strong party near us he can't hide the signs of them from me."

"Can you judge of the number without seeing them?" asked Gardiner, in some surprise.

"Oh, yes."

"How can you do that?"

"Every man to his trade; you know your tactics, and I know mine. I have learned to trail Injuns pretty well in all these years. I couldn't very well explain to you how I do it—there's a knack in it that some men can never pick up. But, to us old forest rangers, there's tongues and voices in the running water, the rustling leaves, the waving grass, and the moss-grown stones. Where an Injun plants his foot he leaves a sign, and though they do their best to hide their trail, there's always eyes keen enough to spy it out."

"I have heard of the wonderful skill you hunters have in following a trail," rejoined Gardiner. "You beat the Indians in their own woodcraft."

"The white man is ahead of the red-man in every respect," replied Glyndon, sententiously. "He can out-run him, out-hunt him, and out-fight him! It's the intellect does it. The Injun's brain-pan wasn't calculated for any thing but a savage—but you can't make the Peace Commissioners believe it. Why don't they pick up all the lazy, good-for-nothing white men in the country, put 'em on a reservation, and feed and clothe them? Waugh! Come, boys, let's see if the 'noble red-man' isn't after our ha'r."

With this contemptuous reflection, Gummery Glyndon threw his long rifle into the hollow of his arm, and walked toward the mouth of the ravine with long strides, followed by the two boys, who kept up with him with some difficulty; but their young hearts bounded with a pleasant excitement.

CHAPTER VI.
FINDING THE TRAIL.

The rapid strides of the old guide carried him half-way across the little valley between the cliffs: then he paused suddenly, and resting the butt of his long rifle upon the ground, and leaning his hands upon its muzzle, took a critical survey of the cliff, where the apparitions had appeared upon the previous night.

"There isn't any way to get up there on this side," he said; "but there may be on the other."

"There's something up there that looks like a hole—a kind of crack in the rock," rejoined Cute. "There may be a cave up there."

"It is a fissure in the cliff, and may extend through to the other side," remarked Percy Vere.

"More'n likely," answered the old hunter. "There's a heap of snow lies on these hills in the winter-time, and the spring thaw sends torrents down to the river, and the water bores its way through the rocks just like a gimlet. These cliffs are a spur of the Cascade Range, and when we get upon the brow of one of them, I think we can see the white peak of Mount Rainier, looking like a big icicle turned the wrong way upwards."

"Is it very high?"

"Thirteen thousand feet, they say. It's the highest peak of the Cascade Mountains."

"Why do they call them *Cascade*?"

"On account of the torrents I was telling you of. I'll show you some grand sights when we get among the mountains, for the road is to run between Mount Adams and Mount Hood, Blaikie told me; that is if Smoholler lets us get any further. We can never get out of this valley with our present force, if he tries to stop us. Let's push on and take the timber there to the right. It's pretty thick at the skirt of the cliff."

The trees fringed the cliff half-way to its summit, a thick growth of spruce, fir, and cedar, and through this the hunter and the boys made their way with some difficulty, as the ground was rocky and uneven, and the dwarf cedars and firs sprung from every crevice of rock and patch of earth.

After a toilsome tramp of an hour they turned the base of the cliff, and emerged upon the other side of it. During their progress they started quite a quantity of game. A huge elk galloped away within easy range, and deer crossed their path several times, while numerous wild-fowl arose from their perches and went whining away.

The temptation to shoot was very great, and it was as much as Glyndon could do to restrain the boys.

"'Tain't safe," he told them. "Wait until we go back. I have an idea that there's Injuns round here, and a rifle-shot would bring 'em on us quicker'n a wink."

"But oh, what a lovely shot that elk was!" cried Percy Vere. "And such splendid horns. I would like to have them for a trophy."

"Wait—there's more of 'em. We must look for Injuns first."

"That's my idea!" cried Cute. "I'd rather have a scalp for a trophy than a pair of horns."

Glyndon smiled, grimly.

"I opine that there's as many scalps around here as horns," he said; "but we must take care we don't lose our own in looking for 'em."

"Have you seen any sign?" asked Percy Vere.

"Not yet; but I think we're coming to it."

They pressed forward, and as they skirted the cliff they bore upward toward its crest. Its aspect was entirely different upon this side, its slope being gradual, and the trees and bushes growing very near to the top.

The way was still difficult. Huge bowlders, some covered with moss and making little openings in the woods, and others thickly studded with fir trees, protruding like green spikes, continually obstructed their way.

"Great Cæsar!" cried Glyndon, pausing to wipe the perspiration from his brow. "This is tough work. I don't see any signs of a trail yet—and there must be one to the top of the cliff, if I could only find it."

Percy Cute, who was the last in the line of march, for he had a natural tendency for loitering, had diverged a little to one side when this halt was made and, though the hunter and Percy Vere were further up the cliff than he was, he had gone more to the right, in a forward direction, and suddenly came upon a kind of open way in the wood.

"Look here!" he called out. "Here's better traveling; come this way."

Glyndon and Percy Vere joined him.

"Why, it looks like a path—a path leading to the summit of the cliff!" cried Percy.

"It is the trail!" said Glyndon, with satisfaction.

He bent over it, and began to examine it attentively, and as he did so his features assumed a grave expression, and he shook his head in a dissatisfied manner.

"Boys!" he said—"I'm an old fool!"

This announcement rather surprised them.

"What's up?" demanded Percy Cute.

"Mischief! We've walked into a trap, and I've led you into it like a consumed idiot as I am."

"How so?" inquired both boys, eagerly.

"Why, don't you see? When we was a looking up at the cliff there must have been one of the red-skins up there watching us. They know we are here in the wood, and they are just waiting for our return to the camp to surprise us. And there's fifty of 'em at least."

The boys were thrown from one surprise into another.

"How can you tell how many there are of them?" asked Percy Vere, curiously.

Glyndon pointed to the trail.

"Here's what tells me," he answered. "These Injuns always go single file, and tread in each other's footsteps to blind their trail, but it would take fifty of 'em, at least, to make so plain a trail. And see there, just at one side, where her foot slipped on the stone, and she stepped out of the trail, heavily, and come near falling—see that broken branch to which she clung to save herself—that tells me there's a squaw along."

The boys were filled with wonder.

"And the trail is scarcely cold either," continued Glyndon, still pursuing his examination. "They passed here less than a half an hour ago, and they're after us."

CHAPTER VII.
A DESPERATE ENCOUNTER.

"After us?" repeated Percy Vere, in some consternation.

"Just so," replied Glyndon, calmly.

"Then we had better git up and 'git,'" suggested Percy Cute. "Let's get back to camp. I wouldn't mind a scrimmage, but I think fifty against three is a leetle too hefty."

"We can't go back the way we came," answered Glyndon. "They're between us and the camp now. We'll have to take to the river the other side of the cliff, and get back that way."

These words revived the boys' spirits.

"Oh! then there is a way out of the trap?" cried Percy Vere.

"I reckon; I never got into so bad a scrape but what I could find a way out of it. Let's travel. We've found out enough, and the quicker we get back to the camp now the better. We know that there is a way up to the cliff's top here, and we've found out that there's a woman in the party, so we can understand something of Smoholler's deviltry last night."

"Yes, but this woman is a squaw, is she not?"

"Of course."

"But the vision that appeared upon the cliff was *white*, how can you account for that?" urged Percy Vere.

Glyndon shook his head in a bewildered manner.

"I can't account for it," he answered, reflectively. "She was white, as you say, and if she wasn't an angel she looked enough like one to be one. The sight of her face affected me strangely—I hain't cried for years, and yet I felt the tears coming as I looked at her. It's witchcraft, and this Injun Prophet just knows how to play it. I don't wonder that the savages think he's something great. I'd like to see him once, just to see what kind of a man he is; but I don't want to see him just now—it might not be wholesome," he added, dryly. "He might lift my ha'r without the formality of an introduction. It's lucky I didn't let you shoot at that elk when you wanted to. The sound of your rifle would have brought the whole squad down upon us."

A peculiar cry arose on the air.

"What's that?" asked Percy Vere; a presentiment of evil entering his mind as he listened to it.

"That's some bird calling for its mate," said Cute.

"Nary a bird," cried Glyndon. "That's an Injun. They've struck our trail, and they're coming for us. Come on; we must get to the river, fast as we can travel."

"Couldn't we make a stand here and fight them?" suggested Percy Vere.

The old hunter shook his head.

"Madness, my boy," he replied. "I like your spunk, but it can't be done. I'm doubtful if we can all get back to the camp, but we'll make a try for it. Our only hope is to make for the river upon the other side of the cliff."

Percy Cute took off his hat, and felt of his hair, while his face assumed a rueful expression.

"I wish I had a photograph of it," he exclaimed.

"Why so?" demanded Glyndon, in some surprise.

"Because I'm afraid that I will never see it again."

Both the hunter and Percy Vere laughed at this sally. This dry humor in the face of threatening danger pleased Glyndon greatly.

"You'll do!" he returned. "Good grit, both of you, and the Injuns shan't get you if I can help it. Come along. We can make a stand at the river's edge, and pepper some of 'em before we take to the water."

They pressed rapidly forward, but their path was beset with many obstacles and obstructions. They had to clamber over huge bowlders, and force their way through thickets of cedar, and fir-trees, nor were brambles wanting in the way.

The numerous signals that now sounded behind them lent spurs to their exertions, for they told them that the Indians were following in swift pursuit.

As they approached the river's brink the wood grew more open; there were less rocks scattered about, and the trees were taller. As they emerged into this opening, with only a fringe of trees between them and the river's bank, the report of guns rattled in quick succession behind them, and a bullet went whistling by Glyndon's ear.

"Great Cæsar!" he cried, "this won't do. Turn at the trees, boys, and prepare for 'em. They'll hit one of us next thing."

They gained a clump of fir trees that grew close together, which afforded them a shelter, and an opportunity to fire their rifles between the trunks.

They were breathless with the exertions they had made, and were only too glad to avail themselves of this temporary rest.

"Phew! that's what I call tall traveling," cried Cute, panting to recover his wind. "I heard the bullets rattling around me like hailstones."

"It's a mercy we were none of us hit," rejoined Percy Vere. "Well, we're lucky so far."

"But we ain't out of it yet," said Glyndon, and he looked grave. "They'll make a rush for us, and when they come, fire your rifles, and then take your pistols. Don't stop to load; if we can't drive 'em back on the first fire, it's all up with us. Give 'em every shot you've got, and then take the river—the current will carry us down to the camp, and we can't be far above it. Maybe they'll hear the firing and be ready to help us."

"Hoop-la!" exclaimed Cute, excitedly. "Here they come. I'll take that big fellow in front."

A wild yell rung through the wood, and a score of painted savages bounded swiftly forward. They had determined upon a desperate charge, evidently; and this mode of attack so different from the customary warfare of the red-man provoked a cry of rage from Glyndon's lips.

"Blast 'em!" he shouted, "somebody's told 'em just how to beat us—but give 'em Jessie! Come on, you murdering thieves!"

The three rifles cracked simultaneously, and two of the advancing warriors went down in their tracks; but Cute missed the tall Indian, the leader of the party, and the savages came on unchecked, like a huge ocean wave. Our three scouts were instantly surrounded. The two boys fought back to back, with revolver and bowie-knife in either hand.

Glyndon clutched his long rifle by the barrel and swept the Indians from his path as he fought his way to the river. He reached the bank and plunged into its turbid tide. He was loth to leave the boys to their fate, but he knew he was powerless to help them—and self-preservation is the first law of nature.

Percy Cute received a blow from a tomahawk that stretched him upon the ground; and Percy Vere found himself clutched by the strong arm of the chief—a hideous-looking object in his war-paint. The warriors drew back, as if feeling that the boy could not cope with his formidable opponent.

Percy's weapons were struck from his hands, and he was hurled to the ground. The hideous face of the savage glared over him, and his knee was pressed upon the boy's chest, nearly suffocating him. Percy gave himself up for lost.

The chief clutched at his throat with his left hand, brandishing his scalping-knife in his right. His fingers came in contact with the ribbon that Percy wore around his neck, and the locket was pulled forth and sprung open.

The chief's eyes fell upon the faces it contained, and a cry of amazement burst from his lips. He sprung to his feet.

A brawny savage was approaching Cute to give him his finishing-blow.

"Hold!" shouted the chief, in a voice that was shrill and loud, like a bugle-call. "Harm him not—harm neither—they are my captives, and their lives are sacred."

A growl of discontent greeted these words.

"Why not kill the pale-face whelps?" cried one of the braves.

The chief stamped angrily upon the ground.

"They are mine, I tell you," he answered, in peremptory tones. "They are the faces I have seen in my visions—and the White Spirit says they are to live."

CHAPTER VIII.
THE PROPHET-CHIEF.

The savages were loth to be cheated of their prey.

"Six of our braves have fallen," replied the warrior who had before spoken, "and the gray hunter has escaped. The blood of our brothers calls for vengeance! Death to the cubs of the pale-face!"

He raised his tomahawk to smite Percy Cute.

"*Monedo! Monedo!*" exclaimed the chief, in that shrill tone which contrasted strongly with the deep guttural of the Indian. "Palsy the arm that strikes against the will of Smoholler!"

The warrior's threatening arm dropped, and he retreated apprehensively from the form of the prostrate boy.

"Smoholler, do not call up your evil-spirit!" he cried, deprecatingly.

The Prophet raised his right arm loftily. Cute recovered in a measure from the effects of the blow which had felled him, and which, fortunately for him, had been given with the blunt end of the tomahawk, and crawled to Percy Vere, who rested upon one knee beneath the Prophet's protecting left arm.

"Are these captives mine?" demanded Smoholler.

A general murmur of affirmation was the response.

"That's right, Smoholler; you're a brick—just you stick to us, that's a good fellow," cried Cute, whose spirits were equal to any emergency. "I say, Percy, our top-knots are safe yet."

This was whispered to his comrade. Percy said nothing; he was gazing in a bewildered manner upon the strange individual who had so unexpectedly spared his life. He was at a loss to account for this sudden clemency.

The Prophet's face, by the aid of war-paint, was made to assume an expression frightful to look upon. He was tall in figure, and appeared to possess extraordinary activity and strength, as indeed he did. Percy thought him the best specimen he had yet seen of an Indian chief. His dress displayed his tall and sinewy form to great advantage. It seemed to have been chosen with the view of producing the greatest effect upon the eye of the beholder.

His moccasins and leggings were of buck-skin, stained black, and trimmed with red fringe. His hunting-shirt was of the same material and color, and trimmed in like manner, and upon its breast was painted in red a grinning fiend, similar to the one who had appeared upon the cliff. His head-dress was the skull of a buffalo, with the horns projecting on either side of his head, and he wore it in the fashion of a helmet.

These projecting, curved horns added to the ferocity of his face, the features of which were nearly indistinguishable beneath the paint with which it was daubed. You could see that he had deep, sunken eyes, with a wild glare to them, like the light of insanity, and a long, prominent nose, and that was all.

Upon his back he wore a mantle of deer-skin, which was curiously stained and colored, and covered with innumerable figures and characters. The prominent figures were a fiend and an angel, who appeared to be engaged in an interminable conflict.

These were representatives of his *Monedos*, or spirits, which his followers firmly believed he could conjure up at will to do his bidding. No wonder the boys gazed with curious eyes upon this strange leader. They could see that he was disposed to befriend them, but they could not understand why.

"The captives are mine; woe to him who seeks to harm them!" cried Smoholler, thus asserting his claim in a manner that proved he considered it settled beyond further dispute. "They shall go to the Rapids with me."

"You're a trump, Smoholler!" exclaimed Percy Cute, gratefully.

"There to be sacrificed to the spirits I control," continued Smoholler.

Cute groaned.

"Oh, law! are we only going out of the frying-pan into the fire?" he muttered.

"Don't be frightened; he does not intend to harm us," whispered Percy Vere.

Cute shook his head in a doleful manner.

"I wish I was sure of that," he answered.

"Well, we can only trust to his mercy."

"Ah, yes! but if he happens to be out of it just now, and can't get a fresh supply?" suggested Cute, lugubriously. He appeared determined to take a discouraging view of the situation. "I know the tricks of these red codgers; I've read about 'em in books. He has got some horrible old idol in a cave up at the Rapids, where he lives, and he makes human sacrifices to it. We shall be grilled, like a couple of innocent lambs, as we are."

"Pshaw! don't lose all your courage at the first reverse. You're not goin to funk, are you?"

"Nary a funk! I'm only taking a rational view of the situation. It's kind of tight papers now, ain't it—you'll allow that?"

"Perhaps; but then we can't help it, can we?"

"No; that's what's the matter!"

"Besides, we can't die but once."

"I know it; that's what makes it so awkward. If a chap could die two or three times he might get used to it, don't you see?"

This reasoning provoked a smile from Percy Vere.

"Well, we must take our chances," he answered. "Repining won't help us. You wanted a brush with the red-skins, and you've had it."

"You bet! My head sings yet where the big chap hit me. It's lucky for me that my skull is tolerably thick. Didn't I see stars when I went down? And I never expected to get up again. Well, we peppered some of 'em, as Gummery would say, and that's some satisfaction. I wonder if he got safe off?"

This question was answered by the return of four of the warriors, who had pursued Glyndon to the river's edge, and who reported that the old hunter had swam down the stream, apparently uninjured by the bullets they had sent after him.

The Prophet turned to Percy Vere.

"What is the number of your party?" he demanded, in good English, and spoken with a purity that surprised the boy.

Percy Vere hesitated to answer this question.

"Speak!" cried the Prophet, in a peremptory manner.

Still Percy Vere hesitated.

CHAPTER IX.
CONJURATION.

"Speak!" repeated the Prophet, and the shrill tones of his voice arose in a menacing manner.

"Why don't you go to our camp, and find out?" suggested Cute, in a sarcastical manner.

"Hush!" cautioned Percy Vere, fearing that the Prophet might become enraged.

"I intend to go," responded the Prophet, coolly. "You see my force here, and you can tell if the surveyors will be able to withstand me." He waved his hand complacently toward his assembled braves. "These are picked warriors. There is enough to drive away the surveyors. But, if more should be wanted, I can summon two hundred more from my village at the Rapids."

Percy Vere glanced at the braves. There was at least forty of them, and each one carried a rifle. Among the friendly tribes through which he had passed he had never seen so fine a body of men. It appeared to him utterly impossible that the surveyors and soldiers could beat back this force.

The Prophet's keen eyes were fixed upon his face, and he read what was passing in his mind by the expression of his features.

"You see how vain it is for your party to struggle against me?" he said.

"Why do you object to the survey being made?" asked Percy. "Why harm people that have no wish to harm you?"

The Prophet drew his tall form proudly up.

"This is my land," he replied, "and I don't want any railroad through it."

"It will not run within a hundred miles of your village."

"I don't want it within a thousand. I am forming a great nation here; already our numbers count by thousands—my followers come from every tribe. I would regenerate the red-man, make him what the Great Spirit intended him to be. These woods teem with game—the water of yonder river is alive with fish. This is the red-man's Paradise, and the white-man is the serpent who would destroy all. Settlement follows the railroad, villages and cities spring up in the wilderness, and then there is no longer any hunting-grounds left for the Indian. The game vanishes from the forest, the fish desert the running streams, and the red-man is left to starve, or become the drudge and servant of the pale-faces."

These words were spoken with a strange eloquence, and thrilled Percy Vere as he listened to them. There was a ring of truth in them that carried conviction to his mind.

"It does appear a hard case for the red-man, I must admit," he rejoined; "but I don't see how you are going to help it. Government lays out these railroads, and they must be built. You can't stop them."

"You will see," replied the Prophet, darkly. "Your party dare not advance after the warning I have given them."

"Perhaps not; but they will remain where they are."

"I will drive them into the river!"

"I do not think you can do so, even with your force. You are not more than four to one against them, and they have fortified their position by this time, and the officer, in command of the soldiers, and the surveyors are brave and determined men. A victory will cost you dear."

These words seemed to impress the chief. He walked moodily backward and forward, for a few moments, in deep thought.

"I must not risk my warriors' lives," he muttered. "I promised them an easy victory, and a defeat would shake their faith in me. Already I have lost six braves, and only those boy captives to show against their loss. I must be cautious in my future movements."

He paused in his walk before Percy Vere, and began to interrogate him again:

"Do you think, if I was to send you back to your party with the assurance that they will not be permitted to advance another foot into this land, that they would abandon their undertaking and depart?" he demanded.

"I do not," replied Percy, promptly.

"Ha! Then you shall go to Priest's Rapids with me. You shall see the wonders of my subterranean temple there; you shall see the chiefs of the Cayuses, Umatillas and Yakimas subservient to my will, and ready at my bidding to make this valley swarm with a red host of painted braves. You shall behold the power of Smoholler, and return to these pale-faced leaders to tell them that at my will I can raise a red war-cloud such as this land has never witnessed, and which will annihilate them when it bursts."

"I say, Percy, old Smo' is a little on the blow," whispered Percy Cute.

The quick ear of the Prophet appeared to catch these words, and he shook his head disdainfully.

"The Tow-head is incredulous," he cried, in the sententious Indian manner; at one moment speaking like a white man and the next with the imagery of the Indian.

Percy Cute opened his mouth in wonder.

"How did he know that I was ever called 'Tow-head?'" he cried.

"Its color is enough to lead him to that conclusion," answered Percy Vere, laughingly.

"If I get out of this scrape, I'll have Ike dye my hair. If I escape a die here, I'll dye in camp," cried Cute.

It was impossible to detect through the paint upon Smoholler's face any indication of what was passing in his mind, for it was like a hideous mask, but Percy Vere thought he was amused by his cousin's drollery.

"Do you also doubt my power?" the Prophet demanded of Percy Vere. "Would it surprise you if I could tell you your name, and the purpose that brings you into this wilderness?"

"It would indeed," answered the boy.

"My spirits can tell me," rejoined the Prophet. "In my dreams the past and future are revealed to me."

He made a few cabalistic motions with his hand, and then assumed a rigid attitude, like one in a trance, his head projected as if awaiting a message from some unseen spirit in the air.

"Whisky is said to be the most potent spirit among the Indians," whispered the irrepressible Cute; "but I don't see any demijohns around here."

"Hush! you will anger him," returned Percy Vere. "It is all a mummery, but we may as well humor it, for our lives depend upon the pleasure of this strange chief."

Smoholler remained rigid, his eyes assuming a vacant look. His braves stood at a respectful distance, leaning upon their rifles, and watching their leader with an intent interest. These dreams of the Prophet were always fraught with singular consequences. They knew he was holding communion with his spirit, who had appeared to them, in the hideous form that was shown upon the cliff, though he generally kept himself invisible.

"*Monedo! Monedo!*" murmured Smoholler, in a resonant whisper.

A dead silence ensued, and the boys, despite their incredulity, were thrilled by a feeling new to them—a sort of supernatural awe.

"*Master, I am here!*"

These words floated above the boys' heads in clear, distinct tones. They clutched at each other's arms, and stared blankly around them. They stood apart with the Prophet; there was not a warrior within a hundred paces of them—not a soul from whom the voice could possibly have proceeded.

"Did you hear that?" gasped Percy Vere.

"I just did," replied Cute, sepulchrally.

"What do you think of it?"

"It knocks me endwise. Hush! he's going to hocus-pocus a little more."

The boys were greatly interested now. Though they felt it was all mummery, they could not help being impressed by it.

The Prophet waved his hand in the direction of the boys.

"Reveal all you know concerning them," he said, as if addressing an invisible spirit above his head—invisible to all other eyes but his.

Then he appeared to listen for a moment; and in this moment the boys could almost hear their hearts beat, in the intensity of their interest in the proceedings. Smoholler nodded his head.

"It is enough, good *Monedo*," he said. "Depart to the Land of Shadows, from whence I summoned you."

Then the Prophet came out of his trance, and addressed himself to the first Percy.

"Your name is Percy Vere," he said. "The locket you wear contains the portraits of your father and your mother. Your companion is your cousin, Percy Cute; and you are here in the wilderness seeking your father."

CHAPTER X.
ONEOTAH.

To say that the boys were surprised by these words would inadequately describe the emotion that seized upon them as they listened to them—they were literally dumbfounded.

"Great heavens! this is wonderful!" cried Percy Vere. "What do you think of it?" he added, appealing to his cousin.

"I take all back; old Smo' is by no means slow!" responded Cute. "I don't wonder that he can bamboozle the benighted Indians, for he has completely kerflummixed me."

The warriors, who had drawn nearer when Smoholler dismissed his spirit, uttered an approving grunt. It may be that the Prophet had purposely availed himself of this opportunity of displaying his divining power before them.

"Is what I have told you true?" he demanded of the boys.

"It is," Percy Vere admitted.

"Every word of it," added Cute. "This beats spirit-rapping all hollow; your spirit comes without a rap, and his information don't cost a rap."

"And having told me so much, I am led to believe you can also tell me where I can find my father?" cried Percy Vere, eagerly.

The Prophet shook his head.

"I can learn from my spirit whether he is alive or dead, perhaps," he replied; "but *Monedo* does not care to seek for a pale-face; he hates the white race, as I do."

"You have a queer way of showing it," exclaimed Cute. "I should have been like poor uncle Ned, without any hair on the top of my head, by this time, if it had not been for you."

"Why have you spared our lives?" asked Percy. "The Indian seldom extends mercy to a captive, I have heard."

The Prophet laughed disdainfully.

"You have heard and read many things about the Indian," he replied; "but they are spoken and written by the pale-faces, and there is little truth in them. I have spared your life that you may bear a message to the surveyor's camp for me. But first you shall partake of food with me. You must feel the need of some refreshment."

"Well, I feel peckish, and no mistake," answered Cute. "So if you have got any fodder, just tote it along."

"Something to eat would not come amiss," said Percy Vere. "We intended to have been back with game to our camp before this."

The Prophet laughed in his forbidding manner.

"Your camp will not get any game on this side of the river," he rejoined. "A dozen of my warriors guard the mouth of the ravine, and it will be sure destruction to the pale-face who attempts to pass through it. You would have fallen into the ambush, had you not turned to the right and ascended the cliff."

"How did you know the direction we had taken?" asked Percy, curiously.

"A sentinel posted upon the cliff gave us warning. Nothing can escape the vigilance of my scouts. They have eyes like hawks. Yonder camp is hemmed in—they must recross the river or I shall drive them into it."

He clapped his hands and an Indian boy came bounding toward him—a boy with a graceful, lithe form, and step as bounding as that of an antelope. He was handsomely dressed, and wore the same colors as the Prophet, and was, evidently, his familiar attendant, or page.

Like the Prophet, he wore a head-dress taken from an animal, but his was the head of an antelope. The sharp horns were left, and the whole face of the animal preserved in such a manner that the boy's face was completely covered by it, and his dark eyes glistened through the eye-holes; and so nicely was the skin fitted to his face, that he appeared to be a boy with an antelope's head.

"Jumping ginger!" exclaimed Cute, as the boy bounded lightly forward; "what kind of a critter is that, anyway?"

"Glyndon was mistaken," remarked Percy, thoughtfully, as he watched the Indian boy's approach.

"In what?"

"It was his tracks we saw. There's no squaw in the party."

"That's so, by king! I never thought of it before; but you are right, there isn't."

"Oneotah," said the Prophet to the boy; "prepare some venison steaks for us."

The boy made a respectful obeisance.

"Yes, master," he replied, in tones that were singularly clear and bell-like, and then he hastened to obey.

Cute smacked his lips.

"Venison-steaks, *a-la-mode de Indian*!" he exclaimed. "I think I can put myself outside of some without any difficulty."

"I must confess to being rather sharp set myself," replied Percy. "That tramp through the thicket, and the lively fight afterward, have freshened up my appetite to a degree."

"The food will be quickly served," said the Prophet. "See, Nature spreads her table for us. Come."

He led the way to a square bowlder that reared its form from the turf beside a little streamlet that went purling by on its way to the river, its clear, crystal water looking cool and refreshing. The Prophet cast himself down beside the rock, and the boys followed his example. As they glanced through the arches of the forest they saw several fires blazing in different directions, and groups of Indians clustered around them. General preparations for a meal were in progress.

The boys were impressed by the romance of the scene, and Cute conveyed his idea of it by exclaiming, rather unpoetically:

"Say, Percy, ain't this high? You said you would like to see Smoholler, the Prophet, and here we are, invited to take an *al fresco* dinner with him."

The Prophet raised himself upon his elbow, and regarded Percy Vere earnestly.

"Why did you wish to see me?" he asked.

"Because I thought you might give me some intelligence of my father," answered Percy.

"Why should you think so?"

"Because you are a man of great intelligence. I heard so before I saw you, and I am satisfied of it now."

The Prophet inclined his head as if pleased with the compliment.

"You possess a wonderful power over the Indians, I can see—and I think few parties of hunters could cross the river, which you watch so jealously, unknown to you."

"You are right; my spies are everywhere, my commands implicitly obeyed. Along the course of yonder mighty river, from its rocky source to where it empties into the ocean, there is no chief who is respected and feared like Smoholler. Already my warriors outnumber the fighting men of the other tribes, and daily I am gaining accessions to my ranks. They come to listen to the recital of my dreams, and they remain, satisfied that the power I profess is not an idle boast. You shall pay me a visit to Priest's Rapids, if you like, and I will show you the germ of a growing nation. Ah! the day will come, and it is not far distant, when the tribes of the Pacific Slope will be gathered into one grand confederacy which will acknowledge Smoholler as its chief."

The Prophet's breast heaved and his eyes dilated with a fervid enthusiasm, as he pronounced these words.

"An Indian emperor!" exclaimed Cute. "Bully for you!"

"And why not? The descendants of the Aztecs and Toltecs still roam these plains and mountains. Why should not I revive the glories of Montezuma's empire?"

"Montezuma's power fell before the white man's advance, and I fear the white settlers crowd too closely upon your projected empire," replied Percy Vere. "But it is a great idea, and that you may prosper is my sincere wish. I would like to see the red-man raised to a better position than that he now occupies. You are the best judge of his capabilities. The white hunters are too prone to regard him in the light of a savage beast—and not without some cause, either."

"Cause? The first offense came from the white man!" cried the Prophet, fiercely.

"It may be so; but, in our particular instance, if you had let us alone, we should not have troubled you."

CHAPTER XI.
A SILVAN REPAST.

The Prophet laughed in that rasping manner so peculiar to him. It was not a pleasant kind of mirth to listen to. It set Percy Cute's teeth on edge every time he heard it.

"You had set foot upon my territory after my warning," he cried. "You know the penalty of trespassing."

"Ah! then you had some hand in the apparitions that appeared upon the cliff last night?"

"They came at my bidding."

At this moment the Indian boy, Oneotah, brought them a venison steak upon a birch platter, some parched corn, and three drinking-horns. He placed the venison and corn before them, and then filled the drinking-horns from the streamlet.

Smoholler did the honors of this silvan table with a courtesy that won strangely upon the boys, and Oneotah stood beside him, ready to do his bidding at the slightest sign.

"What did the surveyors and the soldiers think of the apparitions?" asked Smoholler, after the boys had eaten for a while.

"They were surprised by them," answered Percy.

"Knocked 'em higher'n a kite!" added Cute. "It was a neat piece of hocus-pocus, however you did it. Say, couldn't you give us another squint at that angelic female of yours?"

"The WHITE SPIRIT will come at my bidding," replied the Prophet. "Would you like to see her?" he demanded of Percy Vere.

"Wherefore?" rejoined the youth.

"She might give you intelligence of your father?"

Percy started at this, but shook his head incredulously after a moment's reflection. The Prophet appeared to divine his thoughts.

"You do not believe her to be a spirit?" he asked.

"Candidly, I do not."

"How, then, could she appear upon the face of that inaccessible cliff?"

Percy Vere smiled.

"That is a secret best known to yourself," he rejoined. "At the risk of offending you I must tell you that I believe you to be a skillful Professor of Legerdemain, and by the exercise of it you have gained your ascendancy over the rude minds of the Indians."

"Far from feeling offense, I like your candor," responded the Prophet, graciously. "My power impresses the white mind as well as the red—as you shall have proof anon. You heard the voice of my Monedo, or Spirit, in the air—you heard his voice, but his body remained invisible to your eye. How can you account for that?"

"You may have the gift of ventriloquism. My father had such a gift, for I have often heard my mother describe it. He could throw his voice into inanimate or animate objects to the great perplexity of the hearer."

"Yes," chimed in Cute, "and I have heard lots of funny stories about him. One day an old woman came to the house to make some inquiries, and trod, by accident, upon the cat's tail; and he made the cat say: 'You old fool! don't you know any better than that?' It nearly frightened the old woman into a fit, and she left the house in a big hurry, I tell you; and she believed to her dying day that the cat really spoke to her."

Oneotah indulged in a musical laugh at this recital.

The boys regarded him curiously.

"Holloa! does he understand what I say?" asked Cute.

"Perfectly," replied the Prophet. "English is as familiar to him as his own tongue."

"And to yourself," rejoined Percy Vere, pointedly.

"Yes."

"Do you know I have a suspicion concerning you?"

"Indeed! What is it?"

"I think that you are a white man."

The Prophet laughed.

"Do I look like one?" he returned.

"It is impossible to say what you look like with those hideous daubs of paint upon your face; but you talk like one—and, besides, you are too smart for an Indian."

"Them's my sentiments!" cried Cute. "Smoholler, you beat all the chiefs I ever heard of all hollow."

"Smoholler is the great Prophet of the Snakes," exclaimed Oneotah, fervidly. "Wherever his name is known it is feared and dreaded. His followers are many—his enemies perish, like the withered grass beneath the fire, when his wrath pursues them."

"The boy is one of your converts, I perceive," said Percy, with a smile. "He believes in you."

"He has good cause," answered the Prophet, sententiously. "I saved his life."

"Oh! more than life!" exclaimed Oneotah. "If it was only death that threatened me—"

The Prophet held up his finger warningly, and Oneotah paused and bowed his head submissively.

"Oneotah is Smoholler's slave," he continued. "Until death, or his lips release me, I have sworn to do his bidding."

"Enough! your bondage will not last until death," returned Smoholler, with a significancy which the boys could feel but could not understand. "Be faithful but a short time longer, and you shall be restored to your true condition—and the spirits shall no longer torment you."

The Indian boy appeared to be much gratified by this assurance.

"It is good," he answered. "The heart of Smoholler is noble, he will not deceive me."

Percy Vere was much interested in Oneotah.

"Of what tribe is he?" he asked.

"He was reared by the Nez Perces, but is not of their blood, although he thinks he is," replied Smoholler. "There is a secret concerning his birth, which my skill has divined, and which no other appears to have suspected. He was made captive by a band of Yakimas under a chief named Howlish Wampo, who had surprised and defeated the party to which he was attached. I came up with Howlish Wampo at a critical moment in the boy's fate, and took him away from the chief. Wampo bears me a grudge for it to this day. He would like to gain possession of the boy again, but dare not do so while I protect him. If Oneotah were to rejoin the Nez Perces he would no longer be safe from the pursuit of Howlish Wampo."

Oneotah shuddered, and Percy Vere felt, without exactly understanding why, that there was a covert threat in these words of the Prophet.

"*Multuomah* could protect me," answered Oneotah, plaintively.

"No; not against Howlish Wampo," answered the Prophet, impressively. "Have patience; all I have promised shall come true."

Oneotah bowed his head again in his submissive manner.

"I am content," he answered.

"Why does he wear that antelope's head?" asked Percy Vere.

"To carry out his name."

"You call him the Antelope?"

"Among my followers he is known by that name."

"But the other name—Oneotah?"

"Is one known only to ourselves."

"But it is his true name?"

"Yes."

"But that head is like a mask, it hides his face."

"For that purpose it is worn."

Percy was somewhat surprised by this.

"You do not wish his face to be seen?" he asked.

"No; he has dangerous enemies. None here know him but myself. The shield of my power falls over him, and his influence in my camp is second only to my own. Now, our meal being ended, you shall return to your friends. You have seen a portion of my force, and know my determination. Tell the surveyors and the lieutenant that I will not permit them to advance through the ravine. They must recross the river, or be annihilated. For yourself, if you choose to return, there is a mystic cavern in yonder cliff, and together we will summon the spirits that await my bidding, and seek to learn your father's fate. Will you do so?"

"I will," answered Percy, resolutely.

CHAPTER XII.
THE TREE-LADDER.

Smoholler turned to Oneotah.

"Give me two amulets," he said.

The Antelope boy took two little pouches, made of skin, and richly trimmed with beads, from a kind of large pocket that he wore suspended from a belt around his waist. These were attached to strings made of different-colored strips of doe-skin twisted together. Smoholler gave one to each of the boys.

"Wear these," he said. "They are marked with my totem, and I have charmed them. They are amulets of great power, and they will preserve you from harm. No Indian who knows Smoholler's sign will raise his hand against the wearer of his amulet."

"I thank you for the gift," returned Percy Vere, "and shall always treasure it as the memento of a wonderful man."

"And so shall I," cried Cute. "This will be more efficacious in preserving my top-knot than Professor Ike's Restorative, I'm thinking. Now, how shall we get back to camp? Roll a log into the river and float down upon it, or go back the way we came?"

"There is a trail along the cliff," said Smoholler. "Oneotah will guide you a part of the way. Remember, return this evening, and I will show you a proof of my magical power that will astonish you."

The boys promised to do so, shook hands cordially with the Prophet, notwithstanding his hideous war-paint, and followed Oneotah, who bounded lightly on before.

The way was a rough one, and they had some difficulty in keeping up with Oneotah, who sprung over the bowlders and fallen trees in the path with the nimbleness of a goat.

A toilsome tramp of an hour brought them to a beetling crag that jutted into the water, and appeared to bar all further progress in that direction. Here Oneotah paused, and the boys joined him, panting and breathless.

"Phew! how are we going to get over that?" cried Cute; surveying the impediment in dismay.

Oneotah pointed to a tall spruce tree that grew beside the crag.

"Climb this," he said, "and from its branches you can reach the top of the rock."

"Show! I should never have thought of that."

"Beyond it lies your camp. The descent upon the other side is easy. You can climb?"

"You had better believe it—like a monkey! Good-by, Antelope. Shake hands before we slope."

Oneotah extended his hand cordially, but he winced a little under the vigorous grasp that Percy Cute bestowed upon him, for the fat hands of the boy had quite a degree of strength in them. Cute laughed as Oneotah quickly released his fingers from the roguish squeeze, uttering a suppressed "O—h!"

"Did I hurt you?" asked Cute, with well-assumed innocence.

Oneotah shook his fingers, as if to restore the circulation of the blood in them, by way of answer.

"Don't mind him," cried Percy Vere. "He's always at his tricks. You leave us here?"

"Yes. When you reach the top of this rock you will see your camp."

"Good-by."

Percy extended his hand, but Oneotah hesitated to accept it. Percy laughed.

"Have no fear," he said. "I will not serve you as he did."

Oneotah placed his hand in Percy's, who uttered an exclamation of surprise as he received it.

"No wonder he hurt you," he cried; "why your hand is as soft as a girl's."

Oneotah withdrew his hand quickly.

"I must return to Smoholler," he said. "Come back, and he will show you the Black Spirit and the White. Farewell!"

With these words, he bounded swiftly away, and was soon lost to sight among the trees.

"No wonder he is called the Antelope!" exclaimed Percy Vere, as he gazed after him; "for he is as fleet as one."

"But he ought not be called the Antelope," rejoined Cute.

This difference of opinion, so unusual in friend and cousin, surprised Percy Vere.

"Why not?" he demanded.

"'Tain't correct."

"Indeed! Can you suggest an improvement?"

"Yes; I should call him the Antelopess."

Percy Vere started.

"Why, you don't mean to say—"

"Oneotah is a she antelope—that boy's a girl!"

"I do believe you are right!" returned Percy Vere, with conviction.

"I know I am. Did you not notice how she squealed when I squeezed her hand—and didn't you think her hand was as soft as a girl's?"

"I wish I could have seen her face!" said Percy Vere, thoughtfully.

"That beastly antelope's head hides her face, and is worn on purpose to do so."

"And yet, I fancy, it is a handsome one—it should be to correspond with her shapely and flexible limbs; but I can't imagine why she should wish to hide it."

"That's Smoholler's doings—look at the way he had his face daubed; who could make any thing of his features through all that paint? I tell you what, I don't think the Indians know what she is—the Prophet makes them believe she is a boy, I bet."

"Why should he make her assume such a disguise?"

"Because he's an old humbug! He's up to some trickery to bamboozling these Indians, all the time; that's the way he has made himself a great man out this way. If he had been a white man, he would have been a politician; but as he's red, he turns Prophet—with an eye to profit, don't you see?"

"He certainly has gained a great ascendancy over the Indians."

"Of course he has—there's red fools as well as white ones. He's as smart as a steel trap—you can see that with half an eye. And she's smart."

"Oneotah?"

"Yes; she does just as he says, and believes in him, too, but that's only natural, because I can just guess what she is."

"What?"

"His daughter. She's a chip of the old block, and helps him in his hocus-pocus conjurocus, I'll bet."

"You're good at guessing, and I think your guess is correct."

"You bet! I'm Cute by name, and 'cute by nature. Tell you what, Percy—if we could have taken off that antelope's head, do you know what we would have found beneath it?"

Percy smiled.

"We should have found her face, of course," he answered.

"Yes, and something else—we should have found the face of the Angel that appeared on the cliff, last night."

This assurance surprised Percy Vere.

"Do you think so?" he cried, and his voice was strongly charged with incredulity.

"I'll just bet my bottom dollar on it! She's the Prophet's White Spirit, sure as a gun."

"I have only one objection to urge to that," replied Percy Vere. "The face of the Angel was white—you observed that?"

This remark bothered Cute a little.

"Y-e-s," he admitted.

"And Oneotah is undoubtedly an Indian—whether boy or girl—and his, or her, face must necessarily be red."

"Ah, yes—but couldn't the Prophet whitewash it for the occasion?" cried Cute, triumphantly. "How can we tell but what the Prophet may have found a lot of Lily-white or Pearl Powder in some emigrant train that his braves have plundered?"

"Pshaw! that's too ridiculous an idea."

"You may think so, but I don't. I tell you, this Prophet is a sly old 'coon, and up to all sorts of dodges. And then, how do we know that Oneotah is an Indian girl?" he continued, suddenly inspired with a new idea. "She may be a white girl—stolen away from her home when she was a wee bit of a shaver—I have heard of such things, haven't you?"

"Certainly; the histories of the Indian tribes recount many such instances. I should like to see her face, for what you have said has made me very curious about it."

"You shall see it!"

"How?"

"When we give the Prophet our next call, I'll contrive to throw some flip-flaps for his amusement; and I'll flip flap over Oneotah and knock her head off!"

"Oh! you mustn't hurt her!" remonstrated Percy.

"I don't mean to—I'll only knock the antelope's head off her shoulders, and then you can see her face."

"Do you think you can do it?"

"You just keep your eye on me, and see if I don't. Now, let's shin up this tree and get back to camp. We shall have plenty of news for them."

"Yes; they will be very much surprised to see us, as I think they have given us up for lost. Glyndon has reproached himself with our death, I'm sure, and he will be rejoiced to see us. Come on."

"You first."

They began to climb the tree.

CHAPTER XIII.
MULTUOMAH.

When Gummery Glyndon jumped into the river to escape from his pursuers, he still clutched his trusty rifle by its barrel, and he held fast to it, as the swift current swept him rapidly down-stream.

The Indians did not follow him into the river, but paused upon its bank, and began to hastily reload their guns. The loss they had sustained in their attack upon the hunter and the boys had rendered them furious for vengeance. But the current swept Glyndon out of sight, for the bank was thickly wooded, before they could bring their guns to bear upon him.

They discharged them, notwithstanding, in the direction in which he had gone.

Glyndon laughed as he heard the harmless discharge.

"Trying to shoot me round a corner," he muttered. "Well, they won't get my ha'r this time; but the boys are done for—poor lads! poor lads!"

He shook his gray head sorrowfully over this reflection. Then he saw the trunk of a tree floating in the stream ahead of him. He struck out for it, gained it, and ensconced under its further side, floated with it down the stream. As he went with the current, he made good headway, and soon reached the camp of the surveyors.

A shout from the bank announced that he was observed and recognized as he approached, and the members of the party clustered upon the bank to receive him, as he guided his log toward the shore. At this point the river was fordable, and the banks were sandy and sloping. His feet touched bottom as he came to the sand-bar that stretched across the entire width of the stream, and he allowed the log to float away, and walked ashore.

"What luck?" demanded Lieutenant Gardiner, as the gaunt figure of the old hunter drew near.

"Bad!" answered Glyndon, laconically; and he briefly related to Gardiner, Blaikie and Robbins the particulars of his scout.

All were of his opinion that little mercy would be shown to the boys by their captors, and they deeply lamented their untimely fate.

"Do you know what tribe these Indians belong to?" asked Gardiner.

"They're Smohollers, I reckon," replied Glyndon.

"Did you see him with them?"

"That's more than I can say, for I don't know him. So I might have seen him without knowing it. There was a chief at the head of 'em, and he acted differently from Injun chiefs in general, for he charged right down upon us, without stopping to count the cost, and that was what flaxed us—for they just drew our fire, and were upon us without giving us a chance to reload; and there was too many of 'em for a hand-to-hand fight. I managed to get out of it, but I had to leave the boys. There was no help for it."

The old hunter uttered these words in an exculpatory manner, as if he thought himself responsible, in a measure, for the misfortune that had befallen them.

"This attack looks as if the Indians were determined to prevent us from proceeding in our survey," remarked Robbins.

"That ain't the worst of it," rejoined Glyndon. "They ain't a-going to allow us to stop here long. So just look out for a brush. I hope you have been fixing things here, leftenant," he continued, turning to Gardiner.

"Come and see," replied the lieutenant, who wished to have the old hunter's opinion on the measures he had taken for the protection of the camp.

A semicircular breastwork, composed of felled trees and the loose large stones lying about, had been constructed, running from the river around the grove and back to the river again, completely guarding all approach to the camp, except by the river, which was considered to be protection enough in itself.

Sentinels were posted at different points, and the utmost vigilance observed. The quick discovery of Glyndon's approach was a proof of this; for the river was watched as well as the ravine.

That there was an approach to the camp over the precipitous cliff to the right was a circumstance that Lieutenant Gardiner was yet to learn; not that it made his position more insecure, as his breastwork was some distance from the cliff.

Within the grove, and the breastwork, were the animals and the implements of the party, and Ike Yardell, seeing the probability of remaining there several days, had called upon Corney Donohoe and Jake Spatz to assist him in building a fireplace of stones; a substantial affair that would assist his culinary efforts.

Gummery Glyndon expressed himself highly satisfied with the condition in which the camp had been placed during his absence.

"Smoholler can never drive us out of this," he said. "He don't care much for the lives of his men, that's certain, but he can't take this place in a single charge, and it will cost him pretty dear to try it."

"Have you any idea of the force under his command?" asked Lieutenant Gardiner.

"Nigh onto fifty, I should judge by the looks of his trail."

"We can drive off double that number."

"Yes; but I have an idea that he has a lot more coming. He can set all the other tribes round here against us; and if he should muster three or four hundred warriors in front of us, it would make things look squally for us."

"It would, indeed. They might flank us on the other bank of the river, and so hem us in, and starve us into submission. But I have an idea that this obstruction will only be temporary, and that we shall be permitted to proceed."

"Not a bit of it," replied Glyndon, decidedly. "We have got to whip these Injuns and drive 'em away—that's the only way that we shall ever ever get rid of 'em. And we must have some help to do it."

"What help can we get?"

"Play the old game here, and set Injuns to fighting Injuns. Send for a war-party of the Nez Perces."

"Will they fight against this Indian Prophet?" asked Gardiner, doubtfully.

"They'll fight against the Yakimas, Umatillas, and Cayuses, who are likely to side with him, and if they 'tend to them, we can take care of the Smohollers."

"But where can we find a party of these Nez Perces?"

"There's generally some of 'em at Fort Walla Walla, as their country is the other side of the Blue Mountains. I'm thinking it might be our best plan to go back to the fort, and strengthen our party for a fresh start."

"Or you might go to the fort and see what you could do in the way of obtaining a reinforcement among the friendly Indians," suggested Gardiner. "I am confident that I could hold this position until you return. Let us consult the surveyors, and get their ideas upon the subject."

"Very good—two heads are better than one. Let's have a council of war on the subject. Holloa! What's up now?"

This question was caused by a sudden commotion in the camp, in the direction of the river. They hurried to the bank. A young Indian, whose dress proclaimed him a chief, was riding his horse across the river. He had proclaimed himself a friend to the sentinels, and was suffered to advance unmolested.

"It is Multuomah!" exclaimed Glyndon.

"Do you know him?" asked Gardiner.

"Like a book!—and he's just the man we want, for he's a war-chief of the Nez Perces."

"Good! He is welcome."

The young chief crossed the river, and rode up to the assembled group that awaited his coming. He dismounted with an easy grace, and in a manner that denoted his belief that he was among friends.

"How d'ye do, Multuomah?" cried Glyndon, extending his hand, cordially.

The young chief recognized him pleasantly.

"The Gray Hunter!" he returned, "It is good. He can tell these white men that Multuomah is their friend."

"That's so. You are the youngest chief of the Nez Perces, but you are the smartest one of the lot."

CHAPTER XIV.
THE CHIEF'S BRIDE.

Multuomah inclined his head in a gratified manner at this praise. Lieutenant Gardiner and the surveyors gazed upon him curiously. He was a fine specimen of the warlike nation to which he belonged—the powerful SAHAPTIN tribe. The name of *Nez Perces* was given to this tribe by the early French voyageurs, as a custom once existed among them of wearing a bone ring in the cartilage of the nose, which was pierced for that purpose, hence *Nez Perces*, or in English Pierced Noses; and though the custom is discontinued, the name still remains.

Nor are they the only tribe of the Indians of that section who have lost their original name in the fanciful ones bestowed upon them by the voyageurs, who were the first explorers of the great Northwest. The *Pen D'Oreilles* (Ear-rings), *Cœur D'Alenes* (Needle-hearts), still exist.

Multuomah was of medium hight, slender in figure, but as straight as an arrow, and gracefully proportioned. His face, undisfigured by war-paint, was eminently handsome, and his features wore a pleasant expression. His eyes were dark and keen as an eagle's, and his hair was long and flowing, and as black as jet. His complexion was not unlike bronze in its hue, clear and vivid, and not that dull chocolate hue, so common among the Oregon tribes.

He wore a hunting-shirt, leggins, and moccasins of deer-skin, all richly ornamented with fringe and beads; and an eagle's feather was fastened in the band that kept his long black hair from his eyes. He was armed with rifle, tomahawk, and scalping-knife.

His age could not have been over twenty-five. Take his appearance altogether, he was one of the finest specimens of the red-men to be found at the present day. He had mixed with the white men, and learned some portion of their civilization without becoming contaminated by their vices.

"Is Multuomah alone?" asked Glyndon.

"No," answered the young chief, "there are a hundred warriors awaiting his bidding yonder."

He pointed across the Columbia with a dignified action, but some little pride mingled with his dignity, as if he felt that his consequence would be increased by the announcement of the force at his command. Nor was he deceived in this, for his hearers received the intelligence with great satisfaction.

"Good!" cried Glyndon. "We can wipe the Smohollers out in no time now."

"Is Smoholler near?" asked Multuomah, eagerly.

"Well, he just is. His head-quarters are in yonder cliff, and he has regularly besieged us here."

"Why should he trouble you? Smoholler seldom makes war—though he will always fight stoutly in self-defense."

"He don't like the idea of the railroad going through this territory. These are the surveyors, Multuomah, Mister Blaikie and Mister Robbins, and this is Lieutenant Gardiner, from Fort Walla Walla."

The young chieftain shook hands cordially with all three, as they were introduced to him.

"How many braves has Smoholler with him?" he asked, continuing the conversation with Glyndon.

"Nigh on to fifty, as near as I can calculate from their trail; but me and the boys sent a few of 'em under."

"How was that?"

Glyndon briefly described his scout and skirmish with Smoholler's party.

"The Prophet's men fight bravely, I have been told," rejoined Multuomah.

"You have never had any brush with them?"

"No."

"Then you have got a chance now."

Multuomah shook his head gravely.

"I doubt if my braves will fight against the Prophet," he said; "though I have brought them here for that very purpose."

These words greatly excited the interest of his hearers.

"Then your men believe in the mystical power of this red Prophet?" asked Lieutenant Gardiner.

"Yes; few Indians in this country doubt the power of Smoholler," replied Multuomah. "They dread the spirits that come at his bidding."

"But you—what do you think?"

Multuomah shrugged his shoulders in a dubious manner.

"I do not know what to think," he responded.

"Ah! I see; you would like to doubt him, but can not exactly divest your mind of a certain belief in his supernatural powers. That is not to be wondered at, for he has shown us some astonishing sights since we have been here. I think it's all trickery, but I can't tell how it is done."

Multuomah looked troubled.

"You have seen his spirits?" he asked.

"Yes; black and white. Why should he choose those colors, when he is red?"

"One is the Spirit of Evil; the other the Spirit of Good."

"Have you ever seen them?"

"Never; but I have been told by those who have. It is by means of these spirits that he has gained so great a power. His followers come from all tribes, and their belief in him is great. If I was to attack him, and he should make his spirits appear before my braves, they would fly in terror; and yet there are no braver warriors in all my nation."

The four white men, who were listening to him, exchanged glances.

"This complicates the situation," remarked Blaikie. "I don't see as this reinforcement will, under the circumstances, be of much use to us."

Gardiner and Robbins were of his opinion; but Glyndon took a more favorable view of the matter.

"We must make it of use to us," he cried. "We are strong enough, with Multuomah's band, to just gobble this Prophet, and I'm going to do it. The boys may be alive yet, and we must rescue them."

"But if the chief and his braves dare not fight against Smoholler?" urged Lieutenant Gardiner.

Multuomah crested his head proudly.

"I dare fight against him, and I will," he rejoined. "Multuomah will fight against Smoholler and all his spirits, to gain Oneotah!"

"Oneotah?"

"A squaw?"

These interrogations came from Glyndon and Lieutenant Gardiner. The surveyors smiled and exchanged glances.

"Here's a woman in the case—away out here in the wilderness," said Blaikie. "Who would have thought it?"

"Why not? There are women everywhere," replied Robbins.

Multuomah had nodded his head affirmatively to the questions put to him, and Glyndon now demanded:

"Who is Oneotah, chief?"

"She is the White Lily of our tribe," answered Multuomah, "and she was my promised bride."

"One of your race?"

"No; in her childhood she was captured from the Yakimas by one of our chiefs, who reared her as his own daughter. He named her Oneotah, but, from her fair complexion, she was commonly called the White Lily. She grew to the age of seventeen in our village, and among the many suitors who sought her smiles, her heart gave me the preference."

"I don't wonder at that. You are just the chap to take a girl's eye."

"Our wedding-day was fixed, when she accompanied her adopted father, Owaydotah, upon a hunting expedition. His party was surprised by a band of Yakimas, under the chief Howlish Wampo, and Owaydotah was killed, and Oneotah carried away a captive."

"That was a bad job for you."

"I gave her up for lost, for I knew that Howlish Wampo would make her his wife, inflamed by her great beauty. And he would have done so, had not Smoholler taken her from him."

"What did he do with her?"

Multuomah shook his head sorrowfully.

"I can not tell," he replied. "What I know was told me by a Yakima warrior whom I captured a week ago; but he could not tell me what has befallen Oneotah since Smoholler seized upon her."

CHAPTER XV.
THE OLD HUNTER'S IDEA.

There was a touching plaintiveness to the tone of the Multuomah's voice as he pronounced these words, and his hearers could but sympathize with him in his bereavement.

"Why, this is a kind of turn-about affair," observed Glyndon. "First, you take the girl from the Yakimas, and then they retake her, and then the Prophet puts his finger in the pie. But is the girl really a Yakima?"

"No, I think not."

"I'm glad of that, for I like you, and I don't like the Yakimas. They're mean cusses, and I'd like to see 'em all wiped out. What nation do you think the girl did belong to?"

"Her face was so white that I have often thought she was a daughter of the pale-faces," answered Multuomah.

This reply surprised them all.

"How can that be?" demanded Glyndon.

"She may have been made a captive when a child by the Yakimas in one of their expeditions, either from a settler's cabin or from some emigrant train," rejoined Multuomah. "She understood English when she was brought into our village, and she taught it to me when we were children together."

"That accounts for the ease with which you speak it," remarked Lieutenant Gardiner.

"Yes."

"Your knowledge of our language surprised me, but I can easily understand it now."

Gummery Glyndon had grown very thoughtful.

"We must take this girl from him in spite of his medicine—whether it's quackery or the genuine article," said the old guide, as if coming out of a dream.

Multuomah's dark eyes glistened.

"I came here for that purpose," he answered. "I am willing to dare the Prophet's power—but my braves—"

"You can't count on them, eh?"

Multuomah shook his head doubtfully.

"They will not lift a hand against the Prophet," he replied.

"We can fix that. They wouldn't object to surrounding the Prophet's party, and let us bring him to terms. Just explain to 'em that you want your gal, and that we are going to help you get her. That will make 'em feel all right, I'm thinking."

"They will gain more confidence when they know the soldiers will aid them. They do not fear Smoholler's braves, but his spirits."

"Tell 'em they can not injure the white men."

"That is their belief."

"So much the better! Holloa! what's broke loose now?"

This exclamation was drawn from Glyndon's lips by a shout from one of the sentinels who guarded the breastwork. This shout was taken up by the other soldiers.

"Good heavens! the boys have escaped!" cried Lieutenant Gardiner, excitedly.

Glyndon, usually so placid, found his excitement contagious.

"Great Jericho! it's more'n I expected!" he exclaimed. "I never thought to set eyes on 'em again."

The shout of welcome at their appearance proved the regard in which the boys were held by the soldiers. They approached, rifle in hand, for their weapons had been restored to them by Smoholler when he suffered them to go free, and were overwhelmed with eager inquiries by Glyndon, Lieutenant Gardiner, Blaikie and Robbins.

Percy Vere recounted their adventure with the Prophet, and his narrative was embellished by supplementary remarks from Percy Cute, as he proceeded. Thus they told the story between them.

Their hearers listened to them incredulously; but that the boys stood before them, a living evidence of the truth of their story, they would not have believed it.

"The Prophet let you go?" cried Glyndon.

"As you see," answered Percy Vere.

"Scot free," supplemented Cute; "and give us these gimcracks to protect us from all Indians generally. Nice, ain't they?"

"Amulets!" ejaculated Glyndon, examining them curiously.

"Yes, with the Prophet's tetotum on 'em."

"Totem, you mean."

"Yes, that's it; and we are to tote'em wherever we go, to keep us from harm, according to old Smo'."

"Well, this just beats me," cried Glyndon, in a bewildered manner. "Six of their braves sent to grass, and they let you off. That ain't according to Indian custom, and I can't understand it."

"Smoholler's customs are different from ours," observed Multuomah.

"I should say so!"

Percy Cute took a comprehensive survey of the young chief.

"Holloa! have you taken this young chap prisoner?" he inquired.

"No; he is a friend. This is a Nez Perce chief—Multuomah."

Cute offered his hand cordially to the chief.

"How are you, Multum-in-parvo?" he exclaimed.

Multuomah smiled and shook hands with Cute, who, with his irrepressible spirit of mischief, gave him his favorite hand-squeeze; but Cute was glad enough to withdraw his fat fingers, and dance away with a wry face. The answering squeeze had proved too much for him.

"He's an Odd Fellow!" he remarked, as he straightened out his cramped fingers.

"How do you know that?" asked Percy Vere, enjoying his discomfiture.

"'Cause he's given me the grip."

"Served you right!" cried Glyndon. "No tricks upon travelers. And so you had a long talk with the Prophet?" he added to Percy Vere.

"Yes."

"Did you ask him about your father?"

"I did."

CHAPTER XVI.
HOLDING A COUNCIL.

Glyndon became interested.

"Well, what did he say? Could he tell you any thing about him?"

"Not at that time; but on my return I expect to receive important disclosures from him."

"Return?" cried the old hunter, in astonishment. "Why, you don't calculate to go back to him, do you?"

"Such is my intention."

"Great Jericho! ain't you satisfied with getting off this time, without trying it again?"

"I have the Prophet's word that no injury will befall me."

Gummery Glyndon shook his head dubiously.

"You can't trust to an Injun's word," he said. "They're lyin' cusses, the whole grist of 'em."

"You can trust Smoholler's word," interposed Multuomah. "He will not harm the boys."

"I agree with the chief," remarked Lieutenant Gardiner. "The very fact of his having set them at liberty now is proof enough of that."

"There's something in that," Glyndon admitted. "But didn't Smoholler send us some message, Percy—some intimation to git up and git?"

"He certainly did," replied Percy Vere. "He appears to be resolute that the survey shall not proceed, and he will force us to recross the river, he says, if we do not do so of our own accord. He told me that he should summon more of his warriors from his village at the Rapids, and, if necessary, he would call upon the surrounding tribes to aid him."

"And they will do so," said Multuomah.

"A pretty hornet's nest we appear to have got into here," cried Blaikie.

"And some of the hornets will get snuffed out when they come buzzing around us," responded Glyndon. "We can put an extinguisher on this Prophet, first thing he knows. We'll bottle him up before he can get any help from his own village, or anywhere else. But now, tell me, did you see any squaw with the Prophet?"

"Yes—a squaw called Oneotah!" added Multuomah.

"There, I told you Oneotah was a girl!" cried Cute.

"She is there then?"

This question sprung simultaneously from the lips of Glyndon and Multuomah.

"There is a singular-looking Indian boy there, wearing an antelope's head, which completely conceals his face, whom the Prophet calls Oneotah," replied Percy Vere; "and I have reason to believe that this pretended boy is a girl."

"I'll bet my bottom dollar on it!" exclaimed Cute. "She's got the nicest, softest little fingers that I ever got hold of—"

"You did not see her face?" inquired Glyndon.

"No; the antelope's head conceals it utterly—indeed is worn for the purpose of a disguise, the Prophet himself admitted to me."

"Does she appear to be under any restraint there?" Multuomah now asked, with eager anxiety.

"None whatever. She accompanied us nearly to the camp here, and could have placed herself under its protection, if such had been her desire."

Multuomah's features assumed a troubled expression.

"She is there, then, of her own free will?" he asked, huskily.

"Apparently. Indeed, she seemed to be greatly attached to the Prophet."

"Attached!" stammered Multuomah; and something that sounded very much like a smothered groan burst from his lips.

"He saved her from some great peril, I judge from some words between them that I overheard," continued Percy Vere; "and, now I think of it, it appears to me that your name was mentioned."

"By him?"

"No, first by her. Multuomah, she said, could protect her from some threatening peril."

There was none of the fabled stoicism of the Indian in the young chief as he listened to these welcome words. No white lover ever displayed a more trembling eagerness to learn further intelligence of his sweetheart.

"Ah! she thinks of me—she speaks of me!" he cried. "Smoholler can not then have made her his wife?"

"His wife?" echoed Percy Vere, surprisedly. "No, I do not think there is any such relationship existing between them. The tie that binds her to him appears to be one of gratitude. As I understand it, he appears to have saved her from a ferocious chief of the Yakimas named Howlish Wampo. I remembered the name because it is such an odd one."

"And I have good cause to remember it too," said Glyndon, "for he is the head chief of the murdering tribe that destroyed my home. I heard his name at the time—he was a young chief then, about the age of Multuomah here. It grows upon me—I've got the idea into my head, and it sticks there, that Oneotah is my daughter."

This was a revelation that greatly surprised all, and it made Percy Vere thoughtful.

"She spoke uncommonly good English for an Indian, I thought," he said; "but so did the Prophet, for that matter."

"Tip-top!" affirmed Cute.

"I think the Prophet would give up this girl, if he thought she was your daughter," continued Percy Vere.

Glyndon shook his head dubiously.

"I have my doubts about that," he answered. "These Injuns ain't so fond of giving up any thing they have once got hold of. But I do think we can compel him to give her up."

"You do?" cried Multuomah, eagerly.

"I just do! There's one kind of logic that appeals irresistibly to an Injun, and only one—and that is force. No offence to you, Multuomah. There's good and bad among Injuns, pretty much as there is among white men. Human nature is about the same, no matter what the color of the skin may be. I think we can get this Smoholler into a tight place, and make him squeal!"

"I am of that opinion also," observed Lieutenant Gardiner; "but I would like to have your ideas upon the subject, as an old Indian-fighter. You know the best tactics to adopt against these savages."

By common consent Glyndon found himself constituted the leader of the party. He accepted the position as a matter-of-course, and proceeded to develop his plan of action.

"Well, you see, Leftenant, my idea is just this," he said: "Smoholler doesn't know of the arrival of Multuomah and his Nez Perces, and so he doesn't anticipate any attack from us. He's got a party outlying at the mouth of the ravine yonder, probably a dozen braves, to keep an eye on us, but his main force is on the cliff, where, I opine, there's some kind of a cave."

"Yes; he told me that there was a mystic cavern in the cliff," remarked Percy Vere.

"I thought so. There's a way up to the top, as the trail we found plainly shows. Now you can go to him again, my boy, as he might tell you about your father, and as soon as it gets to be dark we'll move quietly through the ravine, surprise his scouts, and surround the cliff on this side, while Multuomah and his braves cross the river above and unite with us guarding the other side. Then we'll have 'em just like rats in a trap. When he finds out what we are doing you can just tell him that we have been reinforced by a hundred Nez Perces—and mention Multuomah's name, for he must have heard of him—and that we want the girl Oneotah, and will allow him to march off if he gives her up."

"Good!" ejaculated Multuomah.

"The plan appears to be a good one," rejoined Lieutenant Gardiner; "but there is one drawback to it."

"What's that?"

"The Prophet, in his rage at thus finding himself surrounded, might cause the boys to be slaughtered."

The surveyors were also of this opinion, and so said.

"We might obviate that difficulty by keeping the boys here, and make the attack without imperiling them," continued Lieutenant Gardiner.

Percy Vere objected strenuously to this.

"That would deprive me of the opportunity of gaining the knowledge I seek," he urged, "nor would it be fair play to the Prophet."

"Fair play to an Injun—waugh!" rejoined Glyndon, contemptuously.

"Smoholler was very generous toward us," persisted Percy, "and I don't think we ought to take an unfair advantage of him."

"Percy's right," affirmed Cute. "He did the square thing by us, and so give old Smo' a show!"

Blaikie laughed at the boys' earnestness, though his words showed that he was of their way of thinking.

"The Prophet has shown a disposition to keep us back without bloodshed, if he could, as his warnings prove," he said. "I know that but very little faith is to be placed in the tribes hostile to the whites, but this Smoholler may be an exception. He's an uncommon Indian—there's no mistake about that. Now, it appears to me, it would be best to let the boys go to him, learn what they can, and tell him that we have been strongly reinforced—let the Nez Perces light their watch-fires on the opposite bank of the river to that effect—and that he must give up the girl and withdraw his men, or we shall attack him."

Glyndon shook his head, discontentedly.

"That won't work," he said—"I know it won't—there'll be no Smohollers within ten miles of here by morning, and they'll take the girl along with them."

"Let us secure her while we can," cried Multuomah.

"Mr. Blackie's plan is the best," cried Percy; "and I think the Prophet will yield Oneotah up to you, if I tell him you are here."

This assurance surprised them all, and Glyndon received it incredulously.

CHAPTER XVII.
THE BOY EMBASSADORS.

"There's more ways than one to kill a cat," remarked Robbins, bringing his Yankee shrewdness to bear upon this perplexing question. "What's to hinder Multuomah from crossing the river some distance above with half his force, and so prevent the Prophet from retreating back to his village?"

Glyndon brightened up at this suggestion.

"That's the idea, by Jericho!" he exclaimed. "I've always heard that two heads were better than one."

"Even if one is a cabbage-head," supplied Robbins, laughingly.

"I didn't say that—though I don't know whose head you allude to," rejoined Glyndon, with a grim facetiousness. "But you have just hit the idea. Let the boys go. You can give Smoholler a wrinkle of what's in store for him, Percy, if he don't give up the girl; and when you come back safe we'll just wake up these Smohollers lively."

"I am in hopes to bring Oneotah back with me," responded Percy Vere. "There are some good traits in this Prophet, notwithstanding his objection to having a railroad run through his territory. Nor do I believe he can be surprised."

"You don't?"

"No; I think his familiarity with this country will afford him an avenue of escape."

Glyndon shook his head in his dubious manner.

"Not if Multuomah and I get after him," he rejoined. "I think we can make things unpleasant for the Smohollers, eh, chief?"

"If my warriors will second me, he can not escape us," answered Multuomah; "but I prefer that he should give up Oneotah and depart in peace. I have no other cause of quarrel against him."

"But if he will not?" said Blaikie. "If he still persists in obstructing our survey?"

"The Nez Perces will guard your advance, and if they are attacked by the Prophet's braves, they will know how to defend themselves," replied Multuomah. "They believe that the white man has power to break the strength of the Prophet's medicine."

"That's lucky, and they'll fight all the better for it," said Robbins. "Our survey is all right; your party guarantees that. One good turn deserves another, and so we'll do our best to get your girl for you. Let the boys go as embassadors to Smoholler—I don't think they run any risk—and demand the girl, and give him an intimation of what he may expect if he tries to trouble us any further."

Lieutenant Gardiner, Blaikie, and Glyndon were of this opinion, and so the boys prepared for their return to the Prophet. Percy Vere obtained a small branch of a tree to which he affixed a white handkerchief, to serve as a flag of truce. They left the rifles in the camp, but took with them their revolvers and bowie-knives, though they did not think they would have occasion to use either. Thus prepared they left the breastwork, and walked across the open place toward the mouth of the ravine.

The surveyors, the lieutenant, the old hunter and the chief watched the boys curiously, as they walked over this rocky plateau. The sun was sinking, and its declining beams streamed ruddily through the gap in the cliffs, and shed a kind of halo around the boys as they proceeded.

They stepped forward lightly, and with an easy carriage that showed no apprehension of danger lurked in their young hearts.

The watchers behind the breastwork had soon a startling evidence of the vigilance of Smoholler's sentinels. Before the boys reached the mouth of the ravine, a light form sprung from between the rocks and bounded toward them—the form, apparently of an Indian boy, wearing an antelope's head. Oneotah, thus attired, presented a grotesque appearance to the eyes of the beholders. It almost seemed to them as if the animal the head represented was advancing upon its hind-legs, in a series of graceful jumps, to greet the boys.

Oneotah was quickly followed by the tall form of the Prophet, in all his fanciful costume and hideous war-paint. Then, as if by magic, from behind rocks, and from the thickets that skirted the mouth of the ravine, sprung forth a score of Indian warriors, gorgeous in paint and feathers, and the glittering tinsel of their barbaric dress, and each one brandishing a rifle, whose bright barrel glittered in the sunlight.

"Great Jericho! there's a slew of 'em!" cried Glyndon, as he beheld them. "Fifty of 'em, if there's one. Ah! the Prophet's playing a game of brag with us. Wants to show us that he has got enough braves, as he thinks, to wipe us out. He don't know that Multuomah and his Nez Perces are here, that's evident."

Percy Cute was by no means intimidated by this display, for he immediately reversed his position by a hand-spring, and walking toward the Prophet on his hands, offered him one of his feet to shake hands with.

Instead of resenting this action, the Prophet entered into the spirit of it, for he caught Percy Cute by the foot, and with a vigorous motion, that showed his strength of arm, spun the boy up in the air, and Cute descended upon his feet, resuming his proper attitude, and making a bow, after the manner of a gymnast in a circus, as he did so.

During this, Oneotah gave her hand to Percy Vere, and they disappeared together through the mouth of the ravine. Smoholler and Cute followed them, and when the rocks hid them from view, not an Indian warrior was to be seen. They seemed to have melted away among the rocks and trees before which they had been standing, disappearing with a noiseless celerity.

As the tall form of the Prophet, rendered more conspicuous by his richly-bedizened cloak, was lost to view, the sun's rays, which had illuminated this rocky gorge, were suddenly withdrawn, and a gloom, like a pall, settled over the little valley.

The change, though due to natural causes, came so suddenly as to appear peculiar; and the sudden disappearance of the Prophet and his warriors seemed almost supernatural. There is little doubt that the wily chieftain, knowing that the boys' progress through the ravine would be watched by their friends, had artfully arranged the whole scene to make it as impressive as possible upon the minds of the beholders.

If this was indeed the case, the effect produced upon the inmates of the surveyors' camp was all that he could have desired.

As the gloom of night descended, so also did a gloom settle upon Gummery Glyndon's spirits, and he shook his long, gray locks discontentedly.

"There's trickery here, and deviltry, and what not!" he cried. "Why, the Prophet was expecting the boys back—was all ready for them; and yet it was ten chances to one against their trusting themselves in his hands again."

Robbins took a more favorable view of the matter.

"I differ with you there," he said. "He must have seen Percy Vere's great anxiety to learn tidings of his father, and so artfully worked upon his feelings to bring him back to him."

Glyndon shook his head again; but he could not shake away the sudden foreboding that had seized upon his mind.

"Do you think he can tell the boy any thing about his father?" he returned.

"Ah! you are too much for me there; but it is not out of the range of probability. Who knows but what the father came this way, and that Smoholler knows something of his fate?"

Glyndon was impressed by this.

"That's so," he admitted.

"His spirits can tell him," interrupted Multuomah.

The surveyors and Gardiner turned a surprised look upon the young chief.

"Do you believe in his spirits?" they demanded, in a breath.

The young chief smiled.

"Do not you, when you have seen them?" he rejoined.

"It's all a flam!" cried Glyndon. "The only spirit I ever knew an Injun to have is whisky, and they are particularly fond of it. He can't tell the boys any thing that way. You saw the Antelope Boy?" he added, suddenly, impressed by a new idea.

"Yes," answered Multuomah.

"Was it Oneotah?"

"I can not say. Who could tell her in that dress?"

Glyndon shook his head sagely.

"He's fixed her for a purpose that way so nobody can tell her—the boys said as much," he responded.

"She—if it is she—is under no restraint, and does his bidding willingly. He's cast some spell upon her, and that's what he wants of the boys—he'll humbug them to go to his village with him, and make them useful to him. He saw they were smart, and he wants them. His telling them about giving them news of Percy's father is all a humbug."

"Do you think so?" asked Blaikie, surprisedly.

"I just do."

"Then, why did you let them go?"

"I was a dunce to do so! But I kind of thought the Prophet might know something, and then the boys were so anxious to go. However, that can't be helped now; but we must surround the Prophet, and prevent him from carrying them off."

"Let us set about it, and not waste any more time in anticipating an evil that may never occur," suggested Lieutenant Gardiner. "Let Multuomah send half his force over here, and then intercept the Prophet's retreat with the rest. We will wait here until morning, and then force a passage through the ravine. The sound of our rifles will be his signal to advance upon his side. With the force at my disposal, we can soon overpower the Prophet's band."

"Your head's level, leftenant, and that's just what we will do," replied Glyndon; "and now let's have some supper."

CHAPTER XVIII.
THE WHITE LILY.

The Prophet welcomed the boys in that stately manner which was as impressive as it was characteristic with him, and Oneotah placed her soft hand in Percy Vere's with a gentle pressure; but when Cute extended his chubby hand toward her, she declined it expressively.

"Beg to be excused, eh?" said that roguish youngster. "Don't want a repetition of the grip? If I was somebody else now—a certain good-looking young chief—Mister Multuomah."

"Multuomah!" exclaimed Oneotah, tremulously.

The Prophet turned sharply upon Cute.

"What do you know of Multuomah?" he demanded.

Behind the Prophet's back Percy Vere held up his finger, warningly, to his cousin.

"Oh! I don't know much about him," replied Cute, leisurely—"I've seen him, that's all. He's a chief of the Nez Perces—and a splendid looking fellow. He don't daub his face up as you do yours. You put me in mind of the clown in the circus."

The Prophet was not to be put aside in his inquiry. His suspicion had been aroused, and he was determined to satisfy it.

"You have seen Multuomah lately?" he continued, fixing his keen eyes upon Cute's face. "You found him in your camp on your return?"

"Did your spirits tell you that?" rejoined Cute, bewildered by Smoholler's shrewd guess, and endeavoring to dodge the question.

The Prophet shrugged his shoulders.

"Your face tells me so," he answered; "and I have no need to call upon my spirits to corroborate it." He turned to Percy Vere. "Your party has been joined by the young chief of the Nez Perces, Multuomah?" he inquired.

Percy Vere, seeing that Cute had said enough to render any concealment of the truth impolitic, answered:

"Yes."

"You found him there on your return?"

"I did."

"He has come in search of me!" exclaimed Oneotah, joyfully.

This glad cry satisfied Percy Vere that the Antelope Boy was, indeed, a girl, and the promised bride of Multuomah, and, with the inherent chivalry of his nature, he resolved to reunite the lovers.

The Prophet held up his finger warningly to Oneotah.

"No matter how much he seeks for you," he said, "he can never gain possession of you against my will. You know my power—do not provoke it."

Oneotah shuddered and bowed her head submissively.

"Oh! but you will give me to him?" she pleaded.

"When the time comes," he replied, impressively.

She was satisfied with this assurance; and so was Percy Vere.

"That is what I told them!" he cried, impulsively.

The Prophet displayed an eager interest as he resumed his inquiries:

"They spoke of Oneotah? Multuomah seeks her?"

"He does."

"How many warriors has he with him?"

"A hundred."

The Prophet started.

"So many? Did you see them?"

"No; they were upon the other bank of the river. The chief was alone in our camp, in consultation with the lieutenant, the surveyors, and the hunter, Glyndon. They proposed to hem you in, and prevent your retreat. They do not seek to injure you, however; all they wish is to have you give up Oneotah, and allow the survey to proceed."

The Prophet laughed contemptuously.

"And if I should refuse to do either?" he returned.

"They will attack you."

"Fools! The Nez Perces will not fight against Smoholler. When I appear before them, they will scatter like a flock of sheep before the wolf. Multuomah can not take Oneotah from me by force—he had best not attempt it."

Percy, remembering Multuomah's misgivings, was inclined to think that this was no idle boast of the Prophet's.

"I returned to you to arrange matters peaceably, as much as to gain some intelligence of my father, if you can give it to me," he said.

"I can give it to you," replied Smoholler; "but it will try your nerves to receive it, I warn you in advance. You must penetrate with me into the Mystic Cavern beneath yonder cliff—the abode of evil spirits and malignant demons."

"I will do so," rejoined Percy, promptly.

"And so will I," added Cute.

"Good! The sun is already down—let us advance."

The Prophet led the way from the little glen in which they had held this conference, and struck a broad trail leading to the right.

Percy Vere followed the Prophet, Oneotah came next to him, and Cute brought up the rear. In this order they proceeded, the dim light growing dimmer as they advanced.

They had proceeded but a short distance when Percy felt a pressure upon his right arm, and found that Oneotah had come to his side.

"Do not fear the perils of the Mystic Cavern," she said. "The White Spirit will protect you."

These words were uttered cautiously, close to his ear.

"I have no fear," he returned. "I do not think the Prophet will allow his spirits to injure me. I think him a man of his word, and I am in hopes to persuade him to allow you to go to our camp with me on my return."

The grasp upon his arm tightened.

"Oh! if you only can!" she murmured, tremulously.

"You would be glad to see Multuomah again?"

"Yes."

"Oneotah loves Multuomah?"

"Better than her life!"

"Ah! then the Antelope Boy is the White Lily of the Nez Perces?"

"Hush! Oneotah is only the slave of Smoholler—she is only what he pleases until he sets her free," she answered, with a sad resignation.

"And would you remain with him if you had a chance to escape?"

"I must."

"Even if I could restore you to Multuomah?"

"Alas! yes."

The boy could not understand this.

"What tie is it then that binds you so strongly to Smoholler?" he asked, curiously.

"One of gratitude—and still a stronger one."

"What?"

"Hush! don't let him hear us—he is fearful when angered. He is my—"

"Husband?" supplied Percy, remembering the fear that Multuomah had expressed to Glyndon.

"No, no, no!" she answered, quickly. "Why, he is quite an old man. You can not see his features from the war-paint—but I have been permitted to gaze upon his face—I, of all his followers, because I am his *daughter*!"

Percy Vere was thoroughly amazed by this revelation.

"His daughter?" he repeated vaguely.

"Yes. He will give me to Multuomah, in good time, I know he will, for he has always treated me kindly. He saved me from becoming the bride of the fierce chief of the Yakimas. I am not a Nez Perce, nor yet a Yakima, though I have lived with both tribes. I was stolen from my father by the Yakimas when I was a child, and taken from them by a Nez Perce chief named Owaydotah, who reared me as his own daughter. I was very happy in the Nez Perce village, and it was a dreadful blow to me to fall again into the hands of the Yakimas. Smoholler rescued me, and revealed my true history to me, for his Spirit told him where I was. He saved me for Multuomah—can you wonder that I love him for it?"

CHAPTER XIX.
ON THE WAY.

Percy Vere was much interested in what Oneotah had told him, and he gently detained her.

"I do not wonder that you love this strange man," he answered. "I am more and more impressed by the evidences of his power that I have seen. Let him pass on—we can overtake him—you know the way?"

"Oh, yes; these scenes are familiar to me. I have often been here before."

"Yonder cliff is a favorite haunt of the Prophet's, I suppose?"

"Yes."

"You have been in this Mystic Cavern, as you call it?" continued Percy, pursuing his inquiries, curiously.

"Repeatedly."

"And have you never feared the demons who inhabit it?"

Oneotah glanced cautiously before her, as if seeking for the Prophet's tall form, but he had disappeared in the gathering gloom. It was evident that she feared to speak of the cavern and its mysteries in his hearing.

Percy understood the look, and answered to it.

"He is out of sight—he can not hear you," he said. "It appears that you fear this man as well as love him."

"No, I do not fear him; but I would do nothing to displease him."

"Is he easily angered?"

"Oh, no; he has never uttered an angry word to me yet."

Percy smiled.

"It may be because you have been so submissive to his wishes," he rejoined. "You appear to me to have a very amiable temper."

Oneotah laughed, in her musical manner.

"That is why the demons never seek to injure me, I suppose," she answered.

"Have you ever seen any of these demons?" he cried, quickly.

"Yes—one."

"The Black Fiend that appeared to us that night upon the cliff?"

"Yes."

"And he did not seek to injure you?"

"No; why should he?"

Percy shrugged his shoulders; he had a shrewd suspicion of the cause of this immunity, but he did not reveal that suspicion to her.

"True; it must be a fiend indeed that would seek to injure you," he said.

She turned suddenly upon him.

"You like me?" she exclaimed, vivaciously.

"Very much!"

She gave him her hand with frank impulsiveness, crying:

"And I like you!"

"But not so well as Multuomah?" he rejoined, roguishly.

"Multuomah is a great chief!" she replied, sententiously.

"And an Indian of taste!" he added, impressively.

His words bewildered her, for she did not catch his meaning.

"Of taste?" she repeated, in a questioning manner.

"Decidedly!"

"What makes you think so?"

"Don't you?"

She was puzzled again.

"I don't know what you mean," she answered, simply.

He smiled, but, instead of explaining himself, changed the conversation abruptly by asking her:

"You have also seen the White Spirit?"

"I have."

"She is very beautiful!"

"The red-men think her so."

"She has proved a great help to Smoholler in gaining his ascendancy over the minds of the Indians."

"Yes."

"You do not fear *her*?"

"Oh, no; she never injures any one."

"I thought not."

Cute now came up with them.

"What are you stopping here for?" he asked.

"Waiting for you to come up," answered Percy.

"Thank you. I came as fast as I could. I'm short-winded. Phew!"

Cute drew in a long breath, as if preparing for a fresh start.

"That's because you are so fat!" cried Percy, laughingly.

"Fat be blowed!" retorted Cute, indignantly.

"That's what I said—you are blown, because you are so fat."

"Funny, ain't you? Well, I'd rather be fat than a Slim Jim, like you and the Anteloper. Look at his horns! I've often heard of taking a horn, but I wouldn't like to take one of them horns."

Oneotah lowered her head and made a playful butt at Cute, who dodged her nimbly, and got behind Percy, crying out:

"None of that! If you are well-bred, don't be a butter!"

Oneotah laughed merrily at Cute's apprehension.

"That's right, my jolly red boy," continued the fat youth. "And now, Anteloper, don't you think you had better be a sloper? The Prophet has invited us to a lunch, where we can 'sup full of horrors'—a nice little hash of goblins, spooks, demons, ghosts and spirits." Then he began to sing:

"'Red spirits and white, black spirits and gray,

Mingle, mingle, you that mingle may!'"

"Hush!" cried Percy. "You'll scare the owls!"

"The what?"

"The owls!"

"Let 'em scare! Who's afraid? If with my *howls* I scare the owls, let 'em decamp to some adjacent shade!"

"Will you be quiet? I wish to ask Oneotah a few questions before we enter the Mystic Cavern."

Cute clutched Percy suddenly by the arm.

"Will you take a fool's advice?" he asked.

"Well, if I take yours I don't very well see how I can help it," answered Percy quietly.

"Not bad for you, Percy; but fools sometimes hit the truth."

"If you think you can hit it, strike out."

"I was going to suggest that, instead of going into this Mystic Cave, it would be better to cave in on going."

"Pshaw! are you afraid?"

"Not of mortal, red or white, but when it comes to Black Spooks—fellows that fight with their own shinbones, I beg to be excused."

"Nonsense! no harm will come to us."

Cute shook his head, dubiously.

"Oh, won't there?" he cried. "There aren't any Accident Tickets issued on this line yet."

"The Prophet will protect you!" exclaimed Oneotah.

"Then he will be a profit to us if he does. He's as smart as a steel-trap, I know, is Old Smo', so let us go, where glory, or any thing else, awaits us."

"Do be quiet," insisted Percy. "Oneotah was giving me some valuable information when you interrupted us. She says Smoholler is her father."

"I wish I was farther—farther from this!" responded the incorrigible Cute. "It's a wise child that knows its own father, and Antelope may be mistaken. You know what Glyndon thinks; and if she's a she, and belongs to he, how can the other matter be?"

"That is just what I wish to ascertain."

"Fire away then, my boy."

Oneotah did not hear these words. Percy advanced to her, as she had drawn a little apart while the boys held this whispered conference.

"How long have you been with Smoholler, Oneotah?" asked Percy.

"Twelve moons," she answered.

"Good Lord! do you Indian chaps have twelve moons?" cried Cute. "Why, we white fellows only have one!"

"The Indians count time by moons," explained Percy. "Their moons are the same as our months."

"That's for a 'twelve month and a day,' as I have heard the old song say. How moony, and how loony!"

CHAPTER XX.
ONEOTAH'S MEMORIES.

Percy Vere was too much accustomed to Cute's nonsense to pay much heed to it. He continued his inquiries of Oneotah.

"And you were in the power of the Yakima tribe, you say, when he found you—had you been taken a captive by that tribe?"

She nodded assent.

"They took you away from the Nez Perces, but if I remember aright, your infancy was passed among the Yakimas."

"So I told you."

"Do you know how you fell into their hands in the first place?"

"I do not."

They had paused beside a little brook which ran among the rocks, seeking an outlet to the river.

Percy was more and more satisfied that his idea was a correct one, and that the Antelope Boy, or Oneotah, was of white origin. He was tempted to ask her to remove the singular mask she wore, and let him look upon her face, but the thought that she would probably decline to do so restrained him, and he concluded to wait for a better opportunity.

"I am upon the verge of a discovery," he told himself. "I feel convinced of it. The Mystic Cavern will clear away every doubt from my mind. But if this is Glyndon's child, the old hunter should know it; though I dare say he would not have any objection to her marrying this young Nez Perce chief, Multnomah."

This thought led him to resume his questions.

"Your first recollection, then, dates from the Yakima village?" he said.

"Yes," replied Oneotah, answering his questions with great frankness.

"Had you any father there?"

"Not to my knowledge."

"Nor mother?"

"None that ever claimed me."

"Have you any recollection of a mother?"

Oneotah shook her head, pensively.

"No," she answered; "memory recalls no mother's face gently bending over her infant treasure; no father watching with fond delight the playful gambols of his child, tracing in the little face before him the charms of her who was his young heart's choice."

"Nor had you other kindred?"

She shook her head again, with the same plaintive expression.

"I can recall no sister's tenderness, no brother's boisterous love," she rejoined. "Amid the dim phantoms of the past, that recollection brightens into reality, one scene appears the strongest—clearest to my mind."

Percy Vere was much interested in Oneotah's recollections of the past.

"What scene was that?" he asked.

"It was on the plain near where the White Mountain towers to the clouds."

"Mount Rainier?"

"So the white men call it. It was five years ago."

"How old were you then?"

Oneotah reckoned by "moons," but Percy had no difficulty in estimating her age at that period to have been thirteen years.

"It was told to me that, when I grew old enough, I was to be the bride of Howlish Wampo."

"There's a name!" interrupted Cute, who had kept remarkably quiet for him; but the fact was, he was as much interested as Percy in Oneotah's narration. "Who christened him I should like to know? You didn't fancy Mr. Howlish Wampo, eh?"

"I shuddered whenever he looked at me."

"I don't wonder at that, considering your prospect of becoming Mrs. Howlish Wampo. Is he any relative to Wampum?"

"Be quiet!" cried Percy. "Your tongue is like a mill wheel when it once gets started."

"When the wind blows,

Then the mill goes!"

sung Cute.

"You objected, then, to this proposed marriage?" Percy said to Oneotah, continuing his inquiries.

"Yes; and I resolved to escape from him. Chance aided my design. Our little village was surprised by a party of Nez Perces, led by a chief named Owaydotah, and I willingly became his captive."

"He took you to the Nez Perce village?"

"Yes."

"And there you met the young chief, Multuomah?"

Oneotah's voice sunk to a musical whisper as she answered:

"Yes."

Percy smiled, significantly.

"You did not find the same objection to him as to Howlish Wampo?"

"No. I was very happy in the Nez Perce village. But Howlish Wampo was resolved to get me again into his power. When an Indian vows revenge or seeks redress for any injury inflicted upon him he will wait patiently through long years for a favorable opportunity to accomplish his designs. So Howlish Wampo watched and waited, and, at last, a cruel chance made me again his captive."

"He succeeded in surprising you?"

"Yes; and conveyed me back to the Yakima village. Here I was told that I must become his wife. I gave myself up to despair."

"That was a year ago."

"Yes; but when hope had abandoned me, when my dread doom seemed inevitable, Smoholler suddenly appeared in the village. He demanded me of the chief, and Howlish Wampo dared not refuse him."

"That is strange! And the chief yielded you up to Smoholler?"

"He did; for he feared the power of the great Prophet of the Snakes."

"And I don't wonder, for he's a regular anaconda!" interjected Cute. "But won't his Snakeship get tired of waiting for us?"

"True, he will wonder what detains us," answered Oneotah. "Come!"

She led the way up the course of the brook.

"But what plea could Smoholler put forward to claim you?" urged Percy, as he followed her.

"He said I was his child, and that the Yakimas stole me from him."

"He did?"

"Yes."

"And did Howlish Wampo believe him?"

"He must, or he would not have given me up to him."

"That's so. But he can't be your father!" cried Percy, earnestly.

This exclamation surprised Oneotah.

"Why not?" she demanded.

Percy could not very well explain the cause of his doubts to her.

"Because—because," he stammered. "No matter! But do you think he is your father?"

"I do!" she answered, with decision.

CHAPTER XXI.
THE MYSTIC CAVERN.

Percy Vere listened to all this amazedly.

"What makes you think Smoholler is your father?" he asked.

"He has told me so," she replied, simply.

"He may have had a motive in doing so," he urged. "What *proof* have you of it besides his word?"

"A strong one. His face is of the same hue as mine—a hue that neither a Yakima or a Nez Perce possesses."

These words made a powerful impression upon Percy's mind.

"Ha!" he cried, thoughtfully. "I remember Multuomah called you the 'White Lily'—then your face is white?"

"Yes."

"And Smoholler's also?"

"Yes."

Percy became excited.

"Why, then, he is a white man!" he cried.

"I do not know—but he is whiter than any Indian I ever saw."

"He *is* a white man!" affirmed Percy, with conviction. "Good heavens! his evident interest in me—can it be? Your father, girl? No, no—we believe that you are *Glyndon's* daughter; and for the Prophet, he is—"

It was now Oneotah's turn to become amazed.

"What?" she asked, as he paused abruptly.

"No matter; this Mystic Cavern will satisfy my doubts, I fancy. I look forward with interest to the revelations that I shall witness there."

"We have reached its entrance."

"Through this brook?"

"Yes; the spring that feeds it bubbles up within the Mystic Cavern. Take my hand, and give your other hand to your comrade. The entrance is low and narrow."

Cute came up to them as they paused in the rocky bed of the brook. The water was only a few inches deep, and went gurgling along with a pleasant sound.

"Where's the cave?"

"That hole in the rock, where the brook comes through—that is the entrance to it."

"Why, that don't look big enough for a cat to squeeze through."

"It is larger than it appears to be. The water is deeper there, forming a little pool. Come, you must go down upon your hands and knees to enter."

Oneotah set them the example, crawling through the aperture, and they followed her. After proceeding a short distance on their hands and knees, beside the brook (they were not obliged to go in the water, as the stream had worn quite a passage in its long work of ages), they emerged into a spacious and lofty apartment, and found the Prophet awaiting them, holding a flaming torch in his hand.

Its light dimly illuminated the spacious cavern. It was impossible to form any estimate of its size by the light afforded by a single torch. They were in a realm of shadows. Jagged rocks projected upon every side, and an impenetrable gloom was above their heads. The murky air was oppressive to the lungs, and strange murmurs, like the moaning of prisoned spirits, fell upon the ear.

The boys shivered. It appeared to them as if they had entered a huge tomb. Cute's teeth rattled in his head.

"Oh! of all the dismal places!" he muttered.

"Keep up your courage!" urged Percy.

"I'm tryin' to—but I never felt so flunky in all my life. I don't want to play hide-and-seek with red goblins. Ough! it's awful chilly here."

The torchlight made fantastical shadows in the gloom, and it required no great stretch of imagination to fancy that a host of grim goblins surrounded them.

The Prophet stuck his torch in a fissure of the rocky wall.

"Fear nothing," he said. "No harm will befall you. Oneotah and I must not be present when the spirits appear. The White Spirit will obey your bidding. Stand firm—be not appalled at any thing you see. If your father is dead, his spirit will be shown to you."

The Prophet glided away in the gloom, followed by Oneotah. Cute clung convulsively to Percy's arm.

"Let's get out of this," he stammered. "Never mind your father."

"No, I will remain," answered Percy, resolutely. "Don't be frightened—shadows can not harm us."

"Ough! I know it—but who wants to shake hands with a lot of hobgoblins? Oh, Lor'! what's that?"

The torch had dropped from the fissure to the rocky floor. This was the cause of Cute's alarm. It sputtered for a few moments and then expired. Cute dropped upon his knees, as an utter darkness closed about them, clutching Percy around the legs.

"'Now I lay me down to sleep,'" he muttered, his teeth chattering as he did so. "Say your prayers, Percy—we are a couple of lost innocents. Oh! if I ever get out of this—catch me coming here again!"

"Don't be a fool! Where's your courage?"

"I don't know—I think I must have left it outside, for I haven't got it with me."

"Hush! the Spirit is coming!"

"Oh! I wish I was going!"

A light began to appear in a distant part of the cavern, some hundred paces from where they were standing. It increased in volume until it grew vivid, lighting up the cavern with an unearthly luster. Then came a cloud of fleecy smoke, which rolled slowly upward and disclosed the WHITE SPIRIT, standing upon a rocky platform, about three feet from the ground. The light fell strongly upon her face, revealing every feature, and the snowy raiment, the golden bands, the glittering gem upon her forehead, and the faultless contour of the bare limbs. It was a vision of wondrous, supernal loveliness, and Cute's courage revived as he beheld it. He scrambled to his feet, crying out:

"It is the Angel!"

"Angelic, indeed," returned Percy; "and if it is Oneotah, as I shrewdly suspect, I do not wonder that Multuomah loves her."

Cute listened to him surprisedly.

"Oneotah!" he exclaimed. "By Jingo! I think you are right. Now for the Fiend!"

"No; let her show me the spirit of my father, and I will be satisfied."

"*Behold!*" came in a musical whisper, that floated gently toward them.

Again a cloud of smoke arose which hid the White Spirit from view, and when it faded, a different form stood in her place—the form of a tall man, with a pallid visage, and long, flowing black hair. His only dress consisted of a pair of black pants and a white shirt, upon the breast of which was a red gash, from which the blood appeared to be slowly oozing. A look of anguish overspread his features, and with his right hand he pointed to his gory breast, as if intimating that this was the wound that had caused his death.

"MY FATHER!" exclaimed Percy, and he made an involuntary bound toward the figure.

"*Dead!*" came a hoarse whisper.

Percy still pressed forward, dragging Cute, who clung to him in terror, after him, exclaiming, frantically—"Father! father!"

But his feet came in contact with a ridge in the floor, and he and Cute were precipitated to the ground, the latter uttering a despairing yell as he fell. He fell over Percy, and lay a dead weight upon him, and it was only by a strong effort that Percy rolled him off, and struggled to his feet again. But when he did so, light and figure both had disappeared, and the blackness of a starless night encompassed them.

"Gone!" he cried, disappointedly.

"Oh! hocus-pocus conjurocus!" groaned Cute, upon the ground. "Phew! what a smell of brimstone!"

CHAPTER XXII.
THE SEARCH IS ENDED.

In the impenetrable gloom that now surrounded them, Percy could not direct his steps toward the platform on which the figures had appeared. He paused in bewilderment, amazed by what he had beheld.

"It is wonderful!" he exclaimed.

"I hope you are satisfied now," cried Cute.

"I am," returned Percy. "Where are you?"

"Here I am."

Cute arose, and Percy grasped him by the arm.

"A word in your ear," he whispered, impressively. "When they return to us—as they shortly will—and conduct us to a place where there is a fire, as is probable, contrive to knock off Oneota's Antelope head, as you promised to do. You understand?"

"Oh, yes; I'm fly! If she turns out to be the White Angel—"

"Why then, *Smoholler is my father!*"

"Jumping Jerusalem! you don't mean it?"

"I do."

"That accounts for the milk in the cocoanut."

"Hush! I hear footsteps. See, there is the glimmering of a light."

"It is the Antelope with a torch, and her head on, as before. But I'll behead her. Just you wait."

"But don't hurt her."

"Oh, no; I'll decapitate her in the gentlest manner possible."

Oneotah drew near, carrying a torch in her hand. The way in which she had approached proved that the cavern was divided into several apartments, from one of which she had suddenly emerged bearing the torch, whose light revealed her presence.

"Come," she said, as she reached them.

"But tell me—" began Percy.

"No questions now," she interrupted quickly. "This is the Cave of the Shadows—let us leave it for a more cheerful place. Come."

She led the way and the boys followed her, nothing loth to leave that dismal, tomb-like apartment. The way proved a long and winding one, and appeared to be a gradual ascent. Percy Vere could see by the light of Oneotah's torch that they were in a kind of rocky gallery, or subterranean passage, a water-course formerly, though now entirely dry.

After a tedious and tiresome ascent, during which the only words spoken were muttered complaints from Cute as he scraped his shins against projecting rocks, they emerged into a small but comfortable-looking chamber. A fire burned brightly in a natural fire-place in one corner, and as no smoke came into the chamber, it was evident that there was a vent in the rocky roof above that served as a chimney. The light of the fire made the little chamber look cheerful, and disclosed its belongings.

Considerable care had been expended in making it comfortable, and every formation of the rocky chamber had been converted to a useful purpose. Thus a huge square block of stone had been arranged for a table, and smaller stones placed around it to serve as seats. Aromatic bushes had been piled in little odd corners, and were covered with skins to serve as couches. Various weapons were hung upon the walls, mingled with the skins, and skulls, and horns of a variety of animals.

In short, this strange apartment bore a picturesque appearance, and seemed the fit home of a barbaric chief. Nor was the chief wanting, for Smoholler was there; but he had laid aside his head-dress and cloak, and his long black hair, which was almost as thick and as coarse as a lion's mane, hung down upon his shoulders. His face was still disguised in its war-paint, though he appeared to have changed it in some respects since they had last seen him.

He was engaged in a peculiar occupation for a great Prophet and chief, as he was cooking venison steaks before the fire, and the odor of the meat saluted the nostrils of the boys most gratefully.

"By king! this is something like!" exclaimed Cute. "Supper with the Prophet."

Smoholler laughed.

"Boys must eat," he answered. "Have you not heard that the Indians are celebrated for their hospitality?"

"I don't know much about Indians in general," replied Cute, "but you are a particular instance, and hard to beat. I don't think there are many like you."

"Smoholler is the great leader of the red-men," answered the Prophet, sententiously. "In all this land there is no other chief like him."

"That's so!" affirmed Cute. "I'll bet my bottom dollar on you."

Percy Vere, who had been gazing about him, curiously, now said:

"Is not this near the top of the cliff?"

Oneotah placed her torch in a niche in the wall.

"Come," she said.

She gave him her hand, led him into a dark passage, turned abruptly to the right after proceeding a few steps, and checked Percy's further advance. He gazed forward. The sky was overhead, studded with innumerable stars. Far below, down in the gloom of night, a watch-fire sent forth its ruddy glare.

"It is the camp of the surveyors!" he exclaimed, surprisedly.

Oneotah indulged in a musical laugh, as if she rather enjoyed his surprise.

"Yes," she answered.

"And it was here that the White and Black Spirits of Smoholler appeared to us?"

"Yes."

Every thing was becoming plain to him now. He made no other comment, however, but followed Oneotah back into the chamber—the aerie of the Prophet.

The table was soon spread by Oneotah's deft fingers, and they sat down to their repast, the boys finding their appetites well-sharpened by the events of the night. But little was said until their hunger was satisfied, and then Smoholler pushed back his plate, saying:

"What think you of the revelations of the Mystic Cavern? You will be satisfied now to return to your mother and tell her that your father is dead?"

"No, for I think he still lives," returned Percy; and he made Cute a significant gesture toward Oneotah.

"Still lives?" echoed the Prophet.

"Yes; and is known by the name of Smoholler!"

"Jumping Jerusalem!" exclaimed Cute, in pretended amazement, and he made a clutch at one of the horns of the antelope's head, and twitched it dexterously away from Oneotah, revealing her white face, and luxuriant black hair.

"And there is the White Spirit!" continued Percy. "No wonder that you could persuade these ignorant Indians that she is an angel, for she is lovely enough to be one. Father, you will not deny me?"

Smoholler gave him his hand.

"No; for I am proud of such a son," he answered. "You have penetrated my mysteries, but I care not, as I intended to reveal myself to you; but my followers must never know the deceit I have practiced upon them. I have used my chemical knowledge in the manufacture of colored fires with great effect. You have discovered who the angel was; I need scarcely tell you that the Fiend was myself. Oneotah has been my only confederate. And I am likely to lose her, for love has found his way to her heart."

"My father, I will never desert you," cried Oneotah. "I will still be your White Spirit, if you wish it."

"No, Oneotah; you have served my purpose well, and now you shall reap your reward. Your lover, Multuomah, is in yonder camp, and when they return you shall go with them. My power is so well established now that I can do without my White Spirit."

She beamed a grateful smile upon him.

"It will aid your power, father," she cried; "for Multuomah will become your friend, and he will, one day, be the head chief of the Nez Perces."

"True; you see how politic she is; though I must confess that such an alliance has long been one of my calculations."

"Why have you made her think she is your daughter?" asked Percy.

"Because I wanted something to love me; my heart was not satisfied with being feared alone," answered the Prophet, feelingly. "I found her in the power of a brutal savage, and saved her from the degrading fate of becoming his wife. I saw by her face that she was the child of white parents, and so I claimed her as mine."

Oneotah looked disappointed at this revelation.

"Then you are not my father?" she cried.

"No, Oneotah; only by adoption."

"Your real father is in our camp," said Percy. "A hunter, named Glyndon. This, we are all quite assured, is the case."

The Prophet looked surprised. "Is it so?" he asked.

Percy briefly recounted Glyndon's story, as he had repeatedly revealed it to the boys and the lieutenant.

"Undoubtedly she is his daughter," responded Smoholler; "but for her own good, and mine, she had better be considered my daughter."

"I shall never love any other father!" cried Oneotah.

"This seems hard upon Glyndon," remarked Percy.

"Why so? He has long considered her dead. Let him content himself with seeing her happy, and, if he is a sensible man, he will do so. Oneotah, as the supposed daughter of the Great Prophet of the Snakes, will receive a consideration among the Nez Perces that would be denied to her as the daughter of a simple hunter. Besides, it makes a tribe, which has been inclined to be inimical, friendly toward me. I must do all I can to consolidate my power."

"Then you will not return to your home?"

Never. What is past is past. Discussion upon the subject would be idle. Guy Vere is dead, and Smoholler, the Prophet, lives, to found the greatest Indian nation that has ever existed in this country. I will give you gems that will enrich you and your mother for life; but when you leave me, forget me. It will be best. Oneotah shall go with you, and the survey can proceed, for I will no longer obstruct it. I have changed my views concerning the railroad. I think I was wrong in my calculation of the injury it might do me. I shall return to my village at Priest's Rapids. Here are beds at your disposal. Oneotah has her own separate apartment. Let us sleep."

Oneotah withdrew through one of the passages, and the Prophet and the boys disposed themselves upon the couches of skins and fragrant herbs. Sleep came to them speedily.

In the morning they were up with the sun. The Prophet gave Percy a little pouch of deer-skin that contained a fortune in precious stones, and after partaking of a breakfast, and exchanging an affectionate farewell with their strange host, the boys and Oneotah departed. But she no longer wore the boy's dress and antelope's head—she had discarded them for the rich costume of an Indian Princess, for was she not going to her betrothed lord?

I have not space to linger over a description of the surprise that their arrival at the camp created, or the numerous inquiries that were addressed to them.

Glyndon could not determine whether Oneotah was his daughter or not, and she showed no disposition to acknowledge him as a father. She had long considered herself the daughter of the great Smoholler, and, notwithstanding what he had said, she still clung to that belief. Percy saw enough in her face to convince him that she was Glyndon's child, but, under the circumstances, he deemed it best not to interfere in the matter.

Multuomah preferred to receive her as Smoholler's daughter, and conveyed her to his village, where their nuptials were celebrated with great pomp.

Percy Vere and Percy Cute remained with the expedition until the survey was completed, and then returned home.

THE END.

www.ingramcontent.com/pod-product-compliance
Ingram Content Group UK Ltd.
Pitfield, Milton Keynes, MK11 3LW, UK
UKHW031835270325
456796UK00003B/422